Keto Mediterranean Diet Cookbook for Beginners

150 Heart-Healthy Ketogenic Recipes for No-Stress Weight Loss and Lifelong Wellness

Copyright © 2023 by Urban Martin. All rights reserved.

No part of this book may be reproduced or utilized in any form or by any means, electronic or mechanical, including photocopying, recording, or by any information storage and retrieval system, without permission in writing from the publisher, except for brief quotations embodied in critical articles and reviews.

This book is sold subject to the condition that it shall not, by way of trade or otherwise, be lent, resold, hired out, or otherwise circulated without the publisher's prior consent in any form of binding or cover other than that in which it is published and without a similar condition including this condition being imposed on the subsequent purchaser.

While the author has taken every care to ensure the accuracy of the recipes and information presented in this book, readers are advised to use their judgment and consult with a medical professional or a dietary expert if they have specific dietary needs or restrictions. The author and the publisher will not be held accountable for any damage, mishaps, or injury incurred as a result of using the recipes and advice contained herein.

The names, characters, and incidents portrayed in this publication are fictitious. No identification with actual persons (living or deceased), places, buildings, and products is intended or should be inferred.

Make sure to adjust the text according to your needs and consult with a lawyer to ensure your specific requirements are met.

Disclaimer: The content provided is for informational purposes only. It is highly recommended to consult with a lawyer for legal advice.

Table of Contents

- Breakfast Recipes 8
  - Feta Eggs 8
  - Keto Greek Yogurt Smoothie with Cucumber and Mint 8
  - Keto Greek Yogurt Parfait 9
  - Spinach and Feta Crustless Quiche 9
  - Greek Egg and Vegetable Scramble 10
  - Keto Mediterranean Chia Pudding with Berries 10
  - Mediterranean Breakfast Casserole with Artichokes and Olives 11
  - Keto Mediterranean Egg Muffins with Sun-Dried Tomatoes and Olives 11
  - Greek Spinach and Feta Stuffed Mushrooms 12
  - Mediterranean Smoked Salmon and Cream Cheese Roll-Ups 12
  - Greek Frittata with Kalamata Olives and Feta 13
  - Greek Yogurt Parfait with Mixed Nuts and Berries 13
  - Greek-style Baked Omelette with Feta and Tomatoes 14
  - Mediterranean Egg Salad Lettuce Wraps 14
  - Greek Avocado and Tomato Toast 15
  - Mediterranean Breakfast Skewers with Halloumi Cheese and Cherry Tomatoes 15
  - Greek Avocado and Tomato Omelette 16
  - Mediterranean Baked Eggs with Olives and Tomatoes 16
  - Keto Greek Omelette with Spinach, Feta, and Olives 17
  - Greek-style Yogurt and Berry Smoothie 17
- Snacks & Appetizers 18
  - Mediterranean Stuffed Mushrooms 18
  - Greek Salad Skewers 18
  - Cauliflower Hummus with Veggie Sticks 19
  - Keto Mediterranean Antipasto Platter 19
  - Caprese Salad Bites 20
  - Spicy Harissa Shrimp Skewers 20
  - Baked Feta Cheese with Olives and Tomatoes 21
  - Roasted Red Pepper and Feta Dip 21
  - Mediterranean Baked Eggplant Chips 22
  - Olive Tapenade Stuffed Mini Peppers 22
  - Lemon Garlic Roasted Brussels Sprouts 23
  - Mediterranean Cucumber Cups with Tuna Salad 23

- Feta-Stuffed Bacon-Wrapped Dates 24
- Artichoke and Spinach Dip 24
- Marinated Greek Olives 25
- Smoked Salmon Cucumber Roll-Ups 25
- Baked Parmesan Zucchini Chips 26
- Greek Yogurt and Cucumber Dip (Tzatziki) 26
- Stuffed Avocado with Shrimp Salad 27
- Tomato and Mozzarella Skewers with Basil Pesto 27

Meat (Beef, Pork, Lamb, etc.) 28
- Lemon Herb Roasted Pork Tenderloin 28
- Greek-style Stuffed Pork Tenderloin 28
- Moroccan Spiced Ground Beef Stuffed Bell Peppers 29
- Mediterranean Stuffed Bell Peppers 29
- Moroccan Spiced Beef Kabobs 30
- Greek Lemon Chicken Thighs 30
- Herb-Roasted Pork Tenderloin 31
- Grilled Tandoori Chicken Skewers 31
- Rosemary Garlic Roast Beef 32
- Lamb Kofta with Yogurt Sauce 32
- Balsamic Glazed Pork Loin 33
- Spicy Lamb Lettuce Wraps 33
- Mediterranean Stuffed Cabbage Rolls 34
- Garlic Butter Steak with Roasted Vegetables 34
- Grilled Moroccan Spiced Lamb Chops 35

Poultry 36
- Greek Lemon Chicken with Olives 36
- Moroccan Spiced Chicken Skewers 36
- Italian Herb Roasted Chicken Thighs 37
- Keto Greek Chicken Salad 37
- Lemon Herb Grilled Chicken Breast 38
- Oven-Baked Mediterranean Chicken Thighs 38
- Greek Chicken Souvlaki with Feta Cheese 39
- Lemon Garlic Roasted Chicken Drumsticks 39
- Mediterranean Chicken and Vegetable Skillet 40
- Greek Yogurt Marinated Chicken Wings 40

- Mediterranean Chicken and Cauliflower Rice Bowl ... 41
- Italian Baked Chicken Parmesan ... 41
- Lemon Herb Grilled Chicken Skewers ... 42
- Greek Chicken Zoodle Soup ... 42
- Moroccan Chicken Tagine with Olives and Artichokes ... 43

Fish & Seafood ... 44

- Grilled Lemon Garlic Salmon ... 44
- Baked Mediterranean Herb Crusted Cod ... 44
- Lemon Butter Shrimp Skewers ... 45
- Grilled Garlic Butter Lobster Tails ... 45
- Greek Style Baked Tilapia ... 46
- Spicy Garlic Grilled Shrimp ... 46
- Mediterranean Tuna Salad Lettuce Wraps ... 47
- Greek Style Stuffed Squid ... 47
- Baked Lemon Herb Halibut ... 48
- Moroccan Spiced Grilled Swordfish ... 48
- Shrimp and Avocado Salad with Feta ... 49
- Greek Style Grilled Octopus ... 49
- Pan-Seared Scallops with Lemon Caper Sauce ... 50
- Italian Style Grilled Sardines ... 50
- Lemon Dill Baked Cod ... 51
- Greek Shrimp and Zucchini Skillet ... 51
- Mediterranean Style Mussels in Tomato Broth ... 52
- Tuscan Herb Baked Salmon ... 52
- Spicy Garlic Lime Grilled Shrimp Skewers ... 53
- Mediterranean Tuna Stuffed Bell Peppers ... 53

Side dishes ... 54

- Greek Salad with Feta Cheese ... 54
- Roasted Asparagus with Lemon and Parmesan ... 54
- Zucchini Noodles with Pesto ... 55
- Cauliflower Tabbouleh ... 55
- Grilled Eggplant with Tahini Sauce ... 56
- Tomato and Mozzarella Caprese Salad ... 56
- Stuffed Bell Peppers with Ground Turkey and Feta ... 57
- Cucumber and Avocado Salad ... 57

Roasted Brussels Sprouts with Balsamic Glaze 58

Spinach and Feta Stuffed Mushrooms 58

Roasted Red Pepper and Feta Dip 59

Grilled Portobello Mushrooms with Herbed Goat Cheese 59

Greek-style Green Beans 60

Roasted Cauliflower with Garlic and Lemon 60

Mediterranean Roasted Vegetables 61

Artichoke and Tomato Salad 61

Lemon Garlic Roasted Broccoli 62

Marinated Olives and Feta 62

Roasted Garlic and Herb Mushrooms 63

Eggplant and Tomato Stacks with Mozzarella 63

Vegetarian Meals 64

Roasted Eggplant with Feta and Olives 64

Cauliflower Tabbouleh Salad 64

Portobello Mushroom "Steaks" with Herbed Butter 65

Greek Zucchini Fritters with Tzatziki Sauce 65

Spinach and Feta Stuffed Bell Peppers 66

Mediterranean Roasted Vegetable Salad 66

Lemon Garlic Broccoli with Toasted Almonds 67

Ratatouille with Herbed Quinoa 67

Greek Salad with Avocado and Halloumi 68

Zucchini Noodles with Pesto and Cherry Tomatoes 68

Stuffed Artichokes with Herbed Breadcrumbs 69

Cauliflower and Chickpea Curry 69

Mediterranean Stuffed Portobello Mushrooms 70

Greek Spinach and Feta Stuffed Peppers 70

Grilled Halloumi and Vegetable Skewers 71

Mediterranean Roasted Cauliflower with Tahini Sauce 71

Lemon Garlic Roasted Brussels Sprouts 72

Eggplant Parmesan with Zucchini Noodles 72

Greek Lentil Soup with Spinach and Lemon 73

Roasted Asparagus with Feta and Lemon 73

Desserts 74

Lemon Almond Ricotta Cake 74

Raspberry Chia Pudding 74

Chocolate Avocado Mousse 75

Pistachio Rosewater Semolina Cookies 75

Coconut Lime Energy Balls 76

Greek Yogurt Parfait with Berries and Nuts 76

Orange Olive Oil Cake 77

Cinnamon Cardamom Almond Butter Cups 77

Walnut Fig Bites 78

Almond Flour Chocolate Chip Cookies 78

Pomegranate Coconut Panna Cotta 79

Hazelnut Chocolate Truffles 79

Blackberry Almond Crumble Bars 80

Lemon Poppy Seed Muffins 80

Cardamom Pistachio Biscotti 81

Coconut Flour Blueberry Pancakes 81

Orange Almond Biscotti 82

Strawberry Chia Seed Jam 82

Greek Yogurt Lemon Bars 83

Almond Flour Pumpkin Bread 83

Breakfast Recipes

Feta Eggs

Yield: 4 servings | **Prep time:** 5 minutes | **Cook time:** 15 minutes

Ingredients:

- 8 large eggs
- 1/2 cup crumbled feta cheese
- 1/4 cup chopped fresh parsley
- 2 tablespoons olive oil
- 1/2 teaspoon dried oregano
- 1/4 teaspoon garlic powder
- Salt and black pepper to taste
- Optional toppings: sliced cherry tomatoes, chopped Kalamata olives

Directions:

1. Preheat the oven to 350°F (175°C). Grease a baking dish with olive oil.
2. In a medium bowl, whisk the eggs until well beaten.
3. Stir in the crumbled feta cheese, chopped parsley, olive oil, dried oregano, garlic powder, salt, and black pepper. Mix well to combine.
4. Pour the egg mixture into the greased baking dish.
5. If desired, top the mixture with sliced cherry tomatoes and chopped Kalamata olives.
6. Place the dish in the preheated oven and bake for about 15 minutes or until the eggs are set and slightly golden on top.
7. Remove from the oven and let it cool for a few minutes before serving.

Nutritional Information (per serving): Calories: 210 Protein: 16g Carbohydrates: 2g Fat: 15g Fiber: 0g Cholesterol: 410mg Sodium: 460mg Potassium: 200mg

Keto Greek Yogurt Smoothie with Cucumber and Mint

Yield: 2 servings | **Prep time:** 5 minutes | **Cook time:** 0 minutes

Ingredients:

- 1 cup Greek yogurt
- 1 cup cucumber, peeled and chopped
- 1/2 cup fresh mint leaves
- 1/2 cup unsweetened almond milk
- 1 tablespoon lemon juice
- 1 tablespoon Erythritol or your preferred keto-friendly sweetener (optional)
- Ice cubes (optional)

Directions:

1. In a blender, combine the Greek yogurt, cucumber, mint leaves, almond milk, lemon juice, and sweetener (if using).
2. Blend until smooth and creamy. If desired, add ice cubes and blend again until the smoothie reaches your desired consistency.
3. Pour the smoothie into glasses and garnish with additional mint leaves, if desired.

Nutritional Information (per serving): Calories: 105 Protein: 10g Carbohydrates: 6g Fat: 4g Fiber: 1g Cholesterol: 5mg Sodium: 73mg Potassium: 296mg

Keto Greek Yogurt Parfait

Yield: 2 servings | **Prep time:** 10 minutes | **Cook time:** 0 minutes

Ingredients:

- 1 cup full-fat Greek yogurt
- 1/4 cup fresh blueberries
- 1/4 cup fresh strawberries, sliced
- 2 tablespoons chopped walnuts
- 2 tablespoons unsweetened shredded coconut
- 1 tablespoon chia seeds
- Optional: drizzle of sugar-free honey or keto-friendly sweetener

Directions:

1. In two serving glasses or bowls, start by layering half of the Greek yogurt at the bottom of each glass.
2. Add a layer of fresh blueberries on top of the yogurt in each glass.
3. Follow with a layer of sliced strawberries, dividing them evenly between the glasses.
4. Sprinkle each glass with chopped walnuts, unsweetened shredded coconut, and chia seeds.
5. Repeat the layers, starting with the remaining Greek yogurt and continuing with the blueberries, strawberries, walnuts, coconut, and chia seeds.
6. Optionally, drizzle a small amount of sugar-free honey or a keto-friendly sweetener over the top for added sweetness.
7. Serve immediately and enjoy!

Nutritional Information (per serving): Calories: 243 Protein: 16g Carbohydrates: 13g Fat: 15g Fiber: 6g Cholesterol: 10mg Sodium: 59mg Potassium: 311mg

Spinach and Feta Crustless Quiche

Yield: 4 servings | **Prep time:** 15 minutes | **Cook time:** 30 minutes

Ingredients:

- 1 tablespoon olive oil
- 1 small onion, diced
- 2 garlic cloves, minced
- 4 cups fresh spinach leaves
- 1/2 cup crumbled feta cheese
- 4 large eggs
- 1/2 cup heavy cream
- 1/4 teaspoon dried oregano
- Salt and black pepper to taste
- Optional: cherry tomatoes, sliced

Directions:

1. Preheat the oven to 375°F (190°C). Grease a 9-inch pie dish with olive oil.
2. Heat the olive oil in a skillet over medium heat. Add the diced onion and minced garlic. Sauté until the onion becomes translucent.
3. Add the fresh spinach leaves to the skillet and cook until wilted, about 2-3 minutes.
4. Transfer the spinach mixture to the prepared pie dish, spreading it out evenly.
5. Sprinkle the crumbled feta cheese over the spinach.
6. In a separate bowl, whisk together the eggs, heavy cream, dried oregano, salt, and black pepper. Pour the egg mixture over the spinach and feta cheese.
7. If desired, arrange sliced cherry tomatoes on top for added flavor and visual appeal.
8. Bake in the preheated oven for about 25-30 minutes, or until the quiche is set and the top is golden brown.
9. Remove from the oven and let it cool for a few minutes before serving.

Nutritional Information (per serving): Calories: 252 Protein: 13g Carbohydrates: 5g Fat: 20g Fiber: 1g Cholesterol: 240mg Sodium: 317mg Potassium: 351mg

Greek Egg and Vegetable Scramble

Yield: 4 servings | **Prep time:** 10 minutes | **Cook time:** 15 minutes

Ingredients:

- 2 tablespoons olive oil
- 1 small onion, diced
- 1 red bell pepper, diced
- 1 yellow bell pepper, diced
- 2 cups fresh spinach
- 1 cup cherry tomatoes, halved
- 8 large eggs
- 1/4 cup crumbled feta cheese
- 1 tablespoon chopped fresh dill
- Salt and black pepper to taste

Directions:

1. Heat the olive oil in a large skillet over medium heat.
2. Add the diced onion and sauté until it becomes translucent.
3. Add the diced red and yellow bell peppers to the skillet and cook for about 5 minutes, until they start to soften.
4. Stir in the fresh spinach and cherry tomatoes. Cook for another 2-3 minutes until the spinach wilts and the tomatoes soften slightly.
5. In a separate bowl, whisk the eggs together. Season with salt and black pepper.
6. Pour the whisked eggs into the skillet, over the vegetables. Cook and stir gently until the eggs are scrambled and cooked to your desired consistency.
7. Remove the skillet from heat and sprinkle the crumbled feta cheese and chopped fresh dill over the scramble. Toss lightly to combine.
8. Taste and adjust the seasoning if needed.
9. Serve the Greek Egg and Vegetable Scramble hot as a delicious and protein-rich breakfast or brunch option.

Nutritional Information (per serving): Calories: 219 Protein: 15g Carbohydrates: 7g Fat: 15g Fiber: 2g Cholesterol: 372mg Sodium: 273mg Potassium: 503mg

Keto Mediterranean Chia Pudding with Berries

Yield: 4 servings | **Prep time:** 5 minutes | **Cook time:** 0 minutes

Ingredients:

- 1 cup unsweetened almond milk
- 1/4 cup chia seeds
- 1/2 teaspoon vanilla extract
- 1 tablespoon keto-friendly sweetener (e.g., stevia, erythritol)
- 1 cup mixed berries (e.g., strawberries, blueberries, raspberries)
- 2 tablespoons chopped nuts (e.g., almonds, walnuts)

Directions:

1. In a mixing bowl, combine the almond milk, chia seeds, vanilla extract, and keto-friendly sweetener. Stir well to combine.
2. Let the mixture sit for 5 minutes, then stir again to prevent clumping. Repeat this process a few times over the course of 15-20 minutes until the chia seeds have absorbed the liquid and the mixture thickens.
3. Divide the chia pudding evenly into serving jars or bowls.
4. Top the chia pudding with mixed berries and chopped nuts.
5. Refrigerate for at least 2 hours or overnight to allow the chia pudding to set and develop a creamy texture.
6. Serve the Keto Mediterranean Chia Pudding with Berries chilled.

Nutritional Information (per serving): Calories: 139 Protein: 5g Carbohydrates: 12g Fat: 8g Fiber: 9g Cholesterol: 0mg Sodium: 79mg Potassium: 191mg

Mediterranean Breakfast Casserole with Artichokes and Olives

Yield: 6 servings | **Prep time:** 15 minutes | **Cook time:** 40 minutes

Ingredients:

- 8 large eggs
- 1 cup full-fat Greek yogurt
- 1/4 cup unsweetened almond milk
- 1 teaspoon dried oregano
- 1/2 teaspoon dried basil
- 1/2 teaspoon garlic powder
- 1/2 cup crumbled feta cheese
- Salt and black pepper to taste
- 1 can (14 ounces) artichoke hearts, drained and chopped
- 1/2 cup sliced Kalamata olives
- 1/4 cup chopped sun-dried tomatoes
- 1/4 cup chopped fresh parsley

Directions:

1. Preheat your oven to 350°F (175°C) and lightly grease a baking dish.
2. In a large mixing bowl, whisk together the eggs, Greek yogurt, almond milk, dried oregano, dried basil, garlic powder, salt, and black pepper until well combined.
3. Add the chopped artichoke hearts, sliced Kalamata olives, chopped sun-dried tomatoes, and chopped fresh parsley to the egg mixture. Stir gently to evenly distribute the ingredients.
4. Pour the mixture into the greased baking dish and spread it out evenly.
5. Sprinkle the crumbled feta cheese over the top of the casserole.
6. Place the baking dish in the preheated oven and bake for about 35-40 minutes, or until the eggs are set and the top is golden brown.
7. Remove the casserole from the oven and let it cool for a few minutes before slicing and serving.
8. Serve the Mediterranean Breakfast Casserole warm and enjoy a delicious and satisfying start to your day.

Nutritional Information (per serving): Calories: 241 Protein: 17g Carbohydrates: 9g Fat: 16g Fiber: 3g Cholesterol: 321mg Sodium: 632mg Potassium: 376mg

Keto Mediterranean Egg Muffins with Sun-Dried Tomatoes and Olives

Yield: 6 servings | **Prep time:** 10 minutes | **Cook time:** 20 minutes

Ingredients:

- 8 large eggs
- 1/4 cup heavy cream
- 1/4 cup grated Parmesan cheese
- 1/4 cup chopped sun-dried tomatoes
- 1/4 cup sliced Kalamata olives
- 2 tablespoons chopped fresh parsley
- 1/2 teaspoon dried oregano
- Salt and black pepper to taste

Directions:

1. Preheat your oven to 375°F (190°C). Grease a muffin tin or line it with silicone muffin liners.
2. In a mixing bowl, whisk together the eggs and heavy cream until well combined.
3. Add the grated Parmesan cheese, chopped sun-dried tomatoes, sliced Kalamata olives, chopped fresh parsley, dried oregano, salt, and black pepper to the egg mixture. Stir well to evenly distribute the ingredients.
4. Pour the mixture into the prepared muffin tin, filling each cup about 3/4 full.
5. Bake in the preheated oven for approximately 15-20 minutes, or until the egg muffins are set and slightly golden on top.
6. Remove from the oven and let them cool for a few minutes before removing from the muffin tin.
7. Serve the Keto Mediterranean Egg Muffins warm or at room temperature as a delicious and convenient breakfast or snack option.

Nutritional Information (per serving): Calories: 141 Protein: 10g Carbohydrates: 3g Fat: 10g Fiber: 1g Cholesterol: 246mg Sodium: 314mg Potassium: 135mg

Greek Spinach and Feta Stuffed Mushrooms

Yield: 4 servings | **Prep time:** 15 minutes | **Cook time:** 20 minutes

Ingredients:

- 16 large button or cremini mushrooms
- 2 cups fresh spinach, chopped
- 1/2 cup crumbled feta cheese
- 1/4 cup finely chopped red onion
- 2 cloves garlic, minced
- 2 tablespoons chopped fresh dill
- 2 tablespoons extra virgin olive oil
- Salt and black pepper to taste

Directions:

1. Preheat your oven to 375°F (190°C). Line a baking sheet with parchment paper.
2. Remove the stems from the mushrooms and set them aside. Place the mushroom caps on the prepared baking sheet.
3. Finely chop the mushroom stems and transfer them to a mixing bowl.
4. Add the chopped spinach, crumbled feta cheese, finely chopped red onion, minced garlic, chopped fresh dill, extra virgin olive oil, salt, and black pepper to the bowl with the chopped mushroom stems. Mix well to combine.
5. Spoon the spinach and feta mixture into each mushroom cap, pressing it down gently to fill the cavity.
6. Bake in the preheated oven for about 15-20 minutes, or until the mushrooms are tender and the filling is golden brown on top.
7. Remove from the oven and let them cool for a few minutes before serving.
8. Enjoy the Greek Spinach and Feta Stuffed Mushrooms as a flavorful appetizer or side dish.

Nutritional Information (per serving): Calories: 132 Protein: 6g Carbohydrates: 7g Fat: 10g Fiber: 2g Cholesterol: 17mg Sodium: 268mg Potassium: 507mg

Mediterranean Smoked Salmon and Cream Cheese Roll-Ups

Yield: 4 servings | **Prep time:** 10 minutes | **Cook time:** 0 minutes

Ingredients:

- 8 slices smoked salmon
- 4 ounces cream cheese, softened
- 1/4 cup chopped Kalamata olives
- 2 tablespoons chopped fresh dill
- 1 tablespoon capers
- 1 tablespoon lemon juice
- Salt and black pepper to taste

Directions:

1. Lay the smoked salmon slices on a clean surface.
2. In a small bowl, combine the softened cream cheese, chopped Kalamata olives, chopped fresh dill, capers, lemon juice, salt, and black pepper. Mix well until all ingredients are incorporated.
3. Spread a thin layer of the cream cheese mixture onto each smoked salmon slice.
4. Roll up the salmon slices tightly, starting from one end.
5. Once rolled, slice each roll into bite-sized pieces.
6. Arrange the salmon roll-ups on a serving platter.
7. Serve immediately and enjoy the Mediterranean Smoked Salmon and Cream Cheese Roll-Ups as an appetizer or snack.

Nutritional Information (per serving): Calories: 162 Protein: 12g Carbohydrates: 2g Fat: 12g Fiber: 0g Cholesterol: 42mg Sodium: 530mg Potassium: 224mg

Greek Frittata with Kalamata Olives and Feta

Yield: 4 servings | **Prep time:** 10 minutes | **Cook time:** 20 minutes

Ingredients:

- 8 large eggs
- 1/4 cup heavy cream
- 1/2 cup crumbled feta cheese
- 1/4 cup sliced Kalamata olives
- 1/4 cup chopped fresh spinach
- 1/4 cup diced red bell pepper
- 1/4 cup diced red onion
- 2 tablespoons chopped fresh parsley
- 1 tablespoon olive oil
- Salt and black pepper to taste

Directions:

1. Preheat your oven to 375°F (190°C).
2. In a large mixing bowl, whisk together the eggs and heavy cream. Season with salt and black pepper.
3. Heat the olive oil in an oven-safe skillet over medium heat. Add the diced red bell pepper and red onion. Sauté until they start to soften, about 2-3 minutes.
4. Add the sliced Kalamata olives and chopped fresh spinach to the skillet. Cook for an additional 1-2 minutes until the spinach wilts.
5. Pour the egg mixture into the skillet, making sure the vegetables are evenly distributed.
6. Sprinkle the crumbled feta cheese and chopped fresh parsley on top.
7. Transfer the skillet to the preheated oven and bake for 15-20 minutes, or until the frittata is set in the center and lightly golden on top.
8. Remove from the oven and let it cool for a few minutes before slicing.
9. Serve the Greek Frittata with Kalamata Olives and Feta warm or at room temperature.

Nutritional Information (per serving): Calories: 234 Protein: 14g Carbohydrates: 4g Fat: 18g Fiber: 1g Cholesterol: 394mg Sodium: 474mg Potassium: 223mg

Greek Yogurt Parfait with Mixed Nuts and Berries

Yield: 2 servings | **Prep time:** 10 minutes | **Cook time:** 0 minutes

Ingredients:

- 1 cup Greek yogurt
- 1/4 cup mixed nuts (such as almonds, walnuts, and pistachios), chopped
- 1/4 cup fresh berries (such as strawberries, blueberries, and raspberries)
- Optional: drizzle of sugar-free honey or low-carb sweetener for added sweetness
- 1 tablespoon chia seeds
- 1 tablespoon unsweetened shredded coconut
- 1/2 teaspoon vanilla extract

Directions:

1. In a small bowl, combine the Greek yogurt and vanilla extract. Mix well until smooth and creamy.
2. In serving glasses or bowls, layer the Greek yogurt, mixed nuts, fresh berries, chia seeds, and shredded coconut. Repeat the layers until all the ingredients are used, finishing with a sprinkle of mixed nuts and berries on top.
3. Drizzle with sugar-free honey or low-carb sweetener, if desired, for added sweetness.
4. Serve the Greek Yogurt Parfait immediately or refrigerate for later enjoyment.

Nutritional Information (per serving): Calories: 220 Protein: 17g Carbohydrates: 10g Fat: 13g Fiber: 5g Cholesterol: 5mg Sodium: 35mg Potassium: 305mg

Greek-style Baked Omelette with Feta and Tomatoes
Yield: 4 servings | **Prep time:** 10 minutes | **Cook time:** 25 minutes

Ingredients:

- 8 large eggs
- 1/4 cup heavy cream
- 1/2 teaspoon dried oregano
- 1/2 teaspoon dried basil
- Salt and pepper to taste
- 1/2 cup crumbled feta cheese
- 1 cup cherry tomatoes, halved
- 2 tablespoons chopped fresh parsley
- 2 tablespoons olive oil

Directions:

1. Preheat the oven to 375°F (190°C).
2. In a large mixing bowl, whisk together the eggs, heavy cream, dried oregano, dried basil, salt, and pepper.
3. Add the crumbled feta cheese, cherry tomatoes, and chopped parsley to the egg mixture. Stir gently to combine.
4. Heat the olive oil in an oven-safe skillet over medium heat. Make sure the skillet is well-greased to prevent sticking.
5. Pour the egg mixture into the skillet and spread it evenly.
6. Cook for 3-4 minutes, allowing the edges to set.
7. Transfer the skillet to the preheated oven and bake for 20-25 minutes or until the omelette is set in the center and golden brown on top.
8. Remove from the oven and let it cool for a few minutes.
9. Cut the baked omelette into wedges and serve hot.

Nutritional Information (per serving): Calories: 289 Protein: 17g Carbohydrates: 4g Fat: 23g Fiber: 1g Cholesterol: 390mg Sodium: 372mg Potassium: 269mg

Mediterranean Egg Salad Lettuce Wraps
Yield: 4 servings | **Prep time:** 10 minutes | **Cook time:** 10 minutes

Ingredients:

- 6 hard-boiled eggs, peeled and chopped
- 1/4 cup diced cucumber
- 1/4 cup diced red bell pepper
- 1/4 cup diced red onion
- 1/4 cup chopped Kalamata olives
- 2 tablespoons chopped fresh parsley
- 2 tablespoons chopped fresh dill
- 1/4 cup mayonnaise
- 1 tablespoon lemon juice
- Salt and pepper to taste
- 8 large lettuce leaves

Directions:

1. In a mixing bowl, combine the chopped hard-boiled eggs, cucumber, red bell pepper, red onion, Kalamata olives, parsley, and dill.
2. In a separate small bowl, whisk together the mayonnaise and lemon juice. Season with salt and pepper to taste.
3. Pour the mayonnaise mixture over the egg mixture and gently toss until well combined.
4. Place a scoop of the egg salad onto each lettuce leaf.
5. Fold the sides of the lettuce leaf inward and roll it up tightly to form a wrap.
6. Repeat with the remaining lettuce leaves and egg salad.
7. Serve the Mediterranean Egg Salad Lettuce Wraps immediately.

Nutritional Information (per serving): Calories: 256 Protein: 14g Carbohydrates: 5g Fat: 20g Fiber: 2g Cholesterol: 378mg Sodium: 419mg Potassium: 252mg

Greek Avocado and Tomato Toast

Yield: 2 servings | **Prep time:** 10 minutes | **Cook time:** 5 minutes

Ingredients:

- 2 slices of keto-friendly bread
- 1 ripe avocado
- 1 small tomato, sliced
- 2 tablespoons crumbled feta cheese
- 1 tablespoon chopped fresh parsley
- 1 tablespoon lemon juice
- Salt and pepper, to taste
- Extra virgin olive oil, for drizzling

Directions:

1. Toast the slices of keto-friendly bread until crispy.
2. While the bread is toasting, cut the ripe avocado in half, remove the pit, and scoop the flesh into a small bowl. Mash the avocado with a fork until smooth.
3. Stir in the lemon juice, chopped fresh parsley, salt, and pepper into the mashed avocado.
4. Once the toast is ready, spread the avocado mixture evenly onto each slice.
5. Top the avocado spread with sliced tomatoes.
6. Sprinkle crumbled feta cheese on top of the tomatoes.
7. Drizzle a little extra virgin olive oil over the toast.
8. Serve immediately and enjoy!

Nutritional Information (per serving): Calories: 224 Protein: 6g Carbohydrates: 10g Fat: 18g Fiber: 7g Cholesterol: 8mg Sodium: 155mg Potassium: 660mg

Mediterranean Breakfast Skewers with Halloumi Cheese and Cherry Tomatoes

Yield: 4 servings | **Prep time:** 15 minutes | **Cook time:** 10 minutes

Ingredients:

- 8 wooden skewers
- 8 ounces halloumi cheese, cut into cubes
- 16 cherry tomatoes
- 1 tablespoon extra virgin olive oil
- 1 teaspoon dried oregano
- Salt and pepper, to taste
- Fresh basil leaves, for garnish

Directions:

1. Preheat the grill or grill pan over medium heat.
2. Soak the wooden skewers in water for about 10 minutes to prevent them from burning.
3. Thread the halloumi cheese cubes and cherry tomatoes onto the skewers, alternating between them.
4. In a small bowl, whisk together the extra virgin olive oil, dried oregano, salt, and pepper.
5. Brush the olive oil mixture over the skewers, coating them evenly.
6. Place the skewers on the grill or grill pan and cook for about 3-4 minutes per side, or until the cheese is slightly charred and the tomatoes are softened.
7. Remove the skewers from the grill and let them cool slightly.
8. Garnish with fresh basil leaves.
9. Serve the Mediterranean breakfast skewers as a delicious and protein-packed breakfast option.

Nutritional Information (per serving): Calories: 246 Protein: 16g Carbohydrates: 6g Fat: 18g Fiber: 1g Cholesterol: 54mg Sodium: 698mg Potassium: 200mg

Greek Avocado and Tomato Omelette

Yield: 2 servings | **Prep time:** 10 minutes | **Cook time:** 10 minutes

Ingredients:

- 4 large eggs
- 1 tablespoon extra virgin olive oil
- 1/4 cup diced red onion
- 1/2 cup diced tomatoes
- 1/2 avocado, diced
- 1/4 cup crumbled feta cheese
- 2 tablespoons chopped fresh parsley
- Salt and pepper, to taste

Directions:

1. In a bowl, beat the eggs until well combined. Season with salt and pepper.
2. Heat the olive oil in a non-stick skillet over medium heat.
3. Add the diced red onion and sauté for 2-3 minutes, until softened.
4. Add the diced tomatoes and cook for an additional 2 minutes, until slightly softened.
5. Pour the beaten eggs into the skillet and let them cook undisturbed for a few minutes, until the edges start to set.
6. Gently stir the omelette, allowing the uncooked eggs to flow to the bottom of the skillet.
7. Once the eggs are mostly cooked but still slightly runny on top, add the diced avocado, crumbled feta cheese, and chopped fresh parsley on one side of the omelette.
8. Fold the other side of the omelette over the filling and cook for another minute to melt the cheese and warm the avocado.
9. Slide the omelette onto a plate and cut it in half.
10. Serve the Greek avocado and tomato omelette hot, with a side of mixed greens or your favorite keto-friendly accompaniment.

Nutritional Information (per serving): Calories: 294 Protein: 16g Carbohydrates: 9g Fat: 22g Fiber: 5g Cholesterol: 377mg Sodium: 400mg Potassium: 556mg

Mediterranean Baked Eggs with Olives and Tomatoes

Yield: 2 servings | **Prep time:** 10 minutes | **Cook time:** 20 minutes

Ingredients:

- 4 large eggs
- 1 tablespoon extra virgin olive oil
- 1/2 cup diced tomatoes
- 1/4 cup sliced Kalamata olives
- Optional toppings: crumbled feta cheese, chopped fresh basil
- 2 tablespoons chopped fresh parsley
- 1/2 teaspoon dried oregano
- Salt and pepper, to taste

Directions:

1. Preheat the oven to 375°F (190°C). Grease two individual oven-safe dishes with olive oil.
2. In each dish, crack 2 eggs, ensuring the yolks remain intact.
3. Scatter the diced tomatoes and sliced Kalamata olives around the eggs.
4. Sprinkle the chopped fresh parsley and dried oregano over the eggs and vegetables.
5. Season with salt and pepper to taste.
6. Place the dishes in the preheated oven and bake for about 15-20 minutes or until the egg whites are set, but the yolks are still slightly runny.
7. Remove from the oven and let cool for a few minutes.
8. Garnish with optional toppings like crumbled feta cheese and chopped fresh basil.
9. Serve the Mediterranean baked eggs with olives and tomatoes hot, alongside low-carb bread or a side salad.

Nutritional Information (per serving): Calories: 235 Protein: 12g Carbohydrates: 6g Fat: 18g Fiber: 2g Cholesterol: 372mg Sodium: 414mg Potassium: 324mg

Keto Greek Omelette with Spinach, Feta, and Olives

Yield: 2 servings | **Prep time:** 10 minutes | **Cook time:** 10 minutes

Ingredients:

- 4 large eggs
- 1 cup fresh spinach, chopped
- 1/4 cup crumbled feta cheese
- 1 tablespoon olive oil
- 8 Kalamata olives, pitted and sliced
- 1/4 teaspoon dried oregano
- Salt and pepper to taste

Directions:

1. In a bowl, whisk the eggs until well beaten. Season with salt, pepper, and dried oregano.
2. Heat olive oil in a non-stick skillet over medium heat.
3. Add the chopped spinach to the skillet and sauté until wilted, about 2 minutes.
4. Pour the beaten eggs into the skillet, ensuring they cover the entire surface.
5. Cook the omelette for 3-4 minutes or until the edges start to set.
6. Sprinkle the crumbled feta cheese and sliced olives evenly over one half of the omelette.
7. Fold the other half of the omelette over the filling and continue cooking for another 2-3 minutes, or until the eggs are fully set and the cheese has melted.
8. Slide the omelette onto a plate and let it cool for a minute before serving.

Nutritional Information (per serving): Calories: 245 Protein: 17g Carbohydrates: 4g Fat: 18g Fiber: 1g Cholesterol: 405mg Sodium: 570mg Potassium: 285mg

Greek-style Yogurt and Berry Smoothie

Yield: 2 servings | **Prep time:** 5 minutes | **Cook time:** 0 minutes

Ingredients:

- 1 cup Greek yogurt
- 1 cup unsweetened almond milk
- 1 cup mixed berries (such as strawberries, blueberries, and raspberries)
- Ice cubes (optional, for a colder smoothie)
- 1 tablespoon almond butter
- 1 tablespoon chia seeds
- 1 teaspoon honey (optional, for sweetness)

Directions:

1. In a blender, combine the Greek yogurt, almond milk, mixed berries, almond butter, chia seeds, and honey (if using).
2. Blend until smooth and creamy. If desired, add ice cubes and blend again for a colder smoothie.
3. Taste and adjust the sweetness by adding more honey if needed.
4. Pour the smoothie into glasses and serve immediately.

Nutritional Information (per serving): Calories: 210 Protein: 15g Carbohydrates: 15g Fat: 11g Fiber: 6g Cholesterol: 10mg Sodium: 120mg Potassium: 300mg

Snacks & Appetizers

Mediterranean Stuffed Mushrooms

Yield: 4 servings | **Prep time:** 15 minutes | **Cook time:** 20 minutes

Ingredients:

- 24 medium-sized mushrooms
- 1 tbsp olive oil
- 2 cloves garlic, minced
- 1/4 cup chopped sun-dried tomatoes
- Salt and pepper to taste
- 1/4 cup chopped Kalamata olives
- 1/4 cup crumbled feta cheese
- 2 tbsp chopped fresh parsley
- 2 tbsp almond flour

Directions:

1. Preheat oven to 375°F (190°C).
2. Clean mushrooms and remove stems. Set aside caps.
3. Finely chop mushroom stems.
4. Heat olive oil in a skillet over medium heat. Sauté chopped stems and minced garlic for 2-3 minutes.
5. Remove skillet from heat and stir in sun-dried tomatoes, Kalamata olives, feta cheese, parsley, almond flour, salt, and pepper.
6. Stuff each mushroom cap with filling mixture.
7. Place stuffed mushrooms on a parchment-lined baking sheet.
8. Bake for 15-20 minutes until mushrooms are tender and filling is golden brown.
9. Allow mushrooms to cool slightly before serving.

Nutritional Information (per serving): Calories: 120 Protein: 5g Carbs: 7g Fat: 9g Fiber: 2g Cholesterol: 5mg Sodium: 230mg Potassium: 480mg

Greek Salad Skewers

Yield: 4 servings | **Prep time:** 20 minutes | **Cook time:** 0 minutes

Ingredients:

- 1 cup cherry tomatoes
- 1 cup cucumber, cut into chunks
- 1 cup feta cheese, cut into cubes
- 1/2 cup Kalamata olives
- 1/4 red onion, cut into small wedges
- 2 tablespoons extra virgin olive oil
- 1 tablespoon fresh lemon juice
- 1 teaspoon dried oregano
- Salt and pepper to taste
- 4 wooden skewers

Directions:

1. Thread the cherry tomatoes, cucumber chunks, feta cheese cubes, Kalamata olives, and red onion wedges onto the wooden skewers in any desired pattern. Repeat for the remaining skewers.
2. In a small bowl, whisk together the extra virgin olive oil, lemon juice, dried oregano, salt, and pepper to make the dressing.
3. Drizzle the dressing over the Greek salad skewers, ensuring that all the ingredients are evenly coated.
4. Serve immediately and enjoy as a refreshing appetizer or side dish.

Nutritional Information (per serving): Calories: 210 Protein: 9g Carbohydrates: 7g Fat: 16g Fiber: 2g Cholesterol: 30mg Sodium: 520mg Potassium: 240mg

Cauliflower Hummus with Veggie Sticks

Yield: 4 servings | **Prep time:** 15 minutes | **Cook time:** 15 minutes

Ingredients:

- 1 medium cauliflower head, cut into florets
- 3 tablespoons tahini
- 2 cloves garlic, minced
- 2 tablespoons lemon juice
- 2 tablespoons extra virgin olive oil
- 1/2 teaspoon ground cumin
- 1/2 teaspoon paprika
- Salt and pepper to taste
- Assorted vegetable sticks (carrots, cucumbers, bell peppers) for serving

Directions:

1. Steam or boil the cauliflower florets until tender. Drain and let them cool slightly.
2. In a food processor, combine the cooked cauliflower, tahini, minced garlic, lemon juice, extra virgin olive oil, ground cumin, paprika, salt, and pepper.
3. Process the mixture until smooth and creamy, scraping down the sides as needed.
4. Taste and adjust the seasonings according to your preference.
5. Transfer the cauliflower hummus to a serving bowl and refrigerate for at least 30 minutes to allow the flavors to meld together.
6. Serve the cauliflower hummus with assorted vegetable sticks such as carrots, cucumbers, and bell peppers.
7. Enjoy this nutritious and flavorful dip as a keto-friendly snack or appetizer.

Nutritional Information (per serving): Calories: 90 Protein: 3g Carbohydrates: 6g Fat: 7g Fiber: 2g Cholesterol: 0mg Sodium: 60mg Potassium: 320mg

Keto Mediterranean Antipasto Platter

Yield: 4 servings | **Prep time:** 15 minutes | **Cook time:** 0 minutes

Ingredients:

- 4 ounces sliced prosciutto
- 4 ounces sliced salami
- 4 ounces sliced smoked turkey breast
- 4 ounces sliced pepperoni
- 4 ounces sliced mozzarella cheese
- 4 ounces sliced provolone cheese
- Salt and pepper to taste
- 1 cup cherry tomatoes
- 1/2 cup Kalamata olives
- 1/4 cup roasted red peppers, sliced
- 2 tablespoons extra virgin olive oil
- 1 tablespoon balsamic vinegar
- Fresh basil leaves, for garnish

Directions:

1. Arrange the sliced meats, cheeses, cherry tomatoes, Kalamata olives, and roasted red peppers on a platter.
2. In a small bowl, whisk together olive oil, balsamic vinegar, salt, and pepper.
3. Drizzle the dressing over the platter.
4. Garnish with fresh basil leaves.
5. Serve and enjoy as a keto Mediterranean antipasto platter.

Nutritional Information (per serving): Calories: 420 Protein: 28g Carbohydrates: 6g Fat: 32g Fiber: 1g Cholesterol: 80mg Sodium: 1300mg Potassium: 400mg

Caprese Salad Bites

Yield: 4 servings | **Prep time:** 10 minutes | **Cook time:** 0 minutes

Ingredients:

- 16 cherry tomatoes
- 8 small mozzarella balls (bocconcini)
- 16 fresh basil leaves
- Toothpicks, for serving
- 2 tablespoons extra virgin olive oil
- 1 tablespoon balsamic glaze
- Salt and pepper to taste

Directions:

1. Wash and dry the cherry tomatoes and basil leaves.
2. Slice each cherry tomato in half.
3. Drain the mozzarella balls if necessary.
4. Assemble each Caprese Salad Bite by placing a cherry tomato half, a small mozzarella ball, and a fresh basil leaf on a toothpick.
5. Repeat the process for the remaining ingredients.
6. Arrange the Caprese Salad Bites on a serving platter.
7. Drizzle the extra virgin olive oil and balsamic glaze over the bites.
8. Season with salt and pepper to taste.
9. Serve the Caprese Salad Bites as a delicious and refreshing keto Mediterranean appetizer.

Nutritional Information (per serving): Calories: 110 Protein: 6g Carbohydrates: 3g Fat: 8g Fiber: 0g Cholesterol: 20mg Sodium: 90mg Potassium: 120mg

Spicy Harissa Shrimp Skewers

Yield: 4 servings | **Prep time:** 15 minutes | **Cook time:** 10 minutes

Ingredients:

- 1 pound large shrimp, peeled and deveined
- 2 tablespoons harissa paste
- 2 tablespoons extra virgin olive oil
- 2 cloves garlic, minced
- Wooden skewers, soaked in water for 30 minutes
- 1 tablespoon lemon juice
- 1 teaspoon smoked paprika
- 1/2 teaspoon ground cumin
- Salt and pepper to taste

Directions:

1. In a bowl, mix harissa paste, olive oil, minced garlic, lemon juice, smoked paprika, cumin, salt, and pepper.
2. Coat shrimp with the marinade and let them marinate for 10 minutes.
3. Preheat grill or grill pan over medium-high heat.
4. Thread shrimp onto soaked wooden skewers.
5. Grill skewers for 2-3 minutes per side until shrimp turn pink and opaque.
6. Remove from grill and transfer to a serving platter.
7. Garnish with fresh parsley or cilantro if desired.
8. Serve hot as a keto Mediterranean appetizer or main dish.

Nutritional Information (per serving): Calories: 180 Protein: 24g Carbohydrates: 2g Fat: 8g Fiber: 0g Cholesterol: 220mg Sodium: 480mg Potassium: 180mg

Baked Feta Cheese with Olives and Tomatoes

Yield: 4 servings | **Prep time:** 10 minutes | **Cook time:** 20 minutes

Ingredients:

- 8 ounces feta cheese
- 1 cup cherry tomatoes, halved
- 1/2 cup Kalamata olives, pitted and halved
- 2 tablespoons extra virgin olive oil
- Fresh basil leaves, for garnish
- 2 cloves garlic, minced
- 1 teaspoon dried oregano
- Freshly ground black pepper, to taste

Directions:

1. Preheat the oven to 375°F (190°C).
2. Place the feta cheese block in the center of a baking dish.
3. Surround the feta cheese with cherry tomato halves and Kalamata olive halves.
4. Drizzle the extra virgin olive oil over the cheese, tomatoes, and olives.
5. Sprinkle minced garlic and dried oregano evenly over the ingredients.
6. Season with freshly ground black pepper to taste.
7. Bake in the preheated oven for about 20 minutes, or until the feta cheese softens and starts to melt.
8. Remove from the oven and let it cool slightly.
9. Garnish with fresh basil leaves before serving.
10. Enjoy the baked feta cheese with olives and tomatoes as a delicious keto Mediterranean appetizer or side dish.

Nutritional Information (per serving): Calories: 220 Protein: 12g Carbohydrates: 4g Fat: 17g Fiber: 1g Cholesterol: 50mg Sodium: 740mg Potassium: 190mg

Roasted Red Pepper and Feta Dip

Yield: 6 servings | **Prep time:** 10 minutes | **Cook time:** 20 minutes

Ingredients:

- 2 large red bell peppers
- 4 ounces feta cheese, crumbled
- 1/4 cup extra virgin olive oil
- 2 cloves garlic, minced
- Fresh parsley, for garnish
- 1 tablespoon lemon juice
- 1/2 teaspoon dried oregano
- Salt and pepper to taste

Directions:

1. Roast red bell peppers in the oven at 450°F (230°C) for 20 minutes, until charred.
2. Peel, seed, and chop the roasted peppers.
3. Blend roasted peppers, feta cheese, olive oil, minced garlic, lemon juice, dried oregano, salt, and pepper until smooth.
4. Transfer the dip to a serving bowl and garnish with fresh parsley.
5. Serve with keto-friendly crackers or vegetable sticks.

Nutritional Information (per serving): Calories: 140 Protein: 4g Carbohydrates: 4g Fat: 12g Fiber: 1g Cholesterol: 15mg Sodium: 330mg Potassium: 170mg

Mediterranean Baked Eggplant Chips

Yield: 4 servings | **Prep time:** 10 minutes | **Cook time:** 20 minutes

Ingredients:

- 1 large eggplant
- 2 tbsp olive oil
- 1 tsp dried oregano
- Fresh parsley, for garnish
- 1/2 tsp garlic powder
- 1/2 tsp salt
- 1/4 tsp black pepper

Directions:

1. Preheat the oven to 400°F (200°C). Line a baking sheet with parchment paper.
2. Slice the eggplant into thin rounds, about 1/4-inch thick.
3. In a large bowl, combine olive oil, dried oregano, garlic powder, salt, and black pepper. Mix well.
4. Dip each eggplant slice into the olive oil mixture, ensuring both sides are coated.
5. Place the coated eggplant slices in a single layer on the prepared baking sheet.
6. Bake in the preheated oven for 15-20 minutes, or until the eggplant chips are golden brown and crispy.
7. Remove from the oven and let the chips cool slightly.
8. Garnish with fresh parsley.
9. Serve the Mediterranean baked eggplant chips as a healthy and flavorful keto snack or appetizer.

Nutritional Information (per serving): Calories: 90 Protein: 2g Carbohydrates: 7g Fat: 7g Fiber: 4g Cholesterol: 0mg Sodium: 300mg Potassium: 300mg

Olive Tapenade Stuffed Mini Peppers

Yield: 4 servings | **Prep time:** 15 minutes | **Cook time:** 15 minutes

Ingredients:

- 12 mini peppers
- 1 cup pitted Kalamata olives
- 2 cloves garlic
- 2 anchovy fillets (optional)
- Fresh parsley, for garnish
- 2 tbsp capers
- 2 tbsp fresh lemon juice
- 2 tbsp extra virgin olive oil
- 1/4 tsp black pepper

Directions:

1. Preheat the oven to 400°F (200°C). Line a baking sheet with parchment paper.
2. Cut the tops off the mini peppers and remove the seeds and membranes.
3. In a food processor, combine Kalamata olives, garlic cloves, anchovy fillets (if using), capers, lemon juice, extra virgin olive oil, and black pepper. Process until a chunky paste forms.
4. Stuff each mini pepper with the olive tapenade mixture.
5. Place the stuffed peppers on the prepared baking sheet and bake in the preheated oven for 15 minutes, or until the peppers are slightly softened.
6. Remove from the oven and let the stuffed peppers cool slightly.
7. Garnish with fresh parsley.
8. Serve the olive tapenade stuffed mini peppers as a delightful and flavorful keto Mediterranean appetizer.

Nutritional Information (per serving): Calories: 130 Protein: 2g Carbohydrates: 8g Fat: 11g Fiber: 2g Cholesterol: 0mg Sodium: 620mg Potassium: 120mg

Lemon Garlic Roasted Brussels Sprouts

Yield: 4 servings | **Prep time:** 10 minutes | **Cook time:** 20 minutes

Ingredients:

- 1 pound Brussels sprouts
- 2 tbsp olive oil
- 2 cloves garlic, minced
- Zest of 1 lemon
- Fresh parsley, for garnish
- 1 tbsp lemon juice
- 1/2 tsp salt
- 1/4 tsp black pepper

Directions:

1. Preheat the oven to 425°F (220°C). Line a baking sheet with parchment paper.
2. Trim the ends of the Brussels sprouts and remove any outer leaves that are wilted or damaged. Cut larger sprouts in half.
3. In a large bowl, combine olive oil, minced garlic, lemon zest, lemon juice, salt, and black pepper. Mix well.
4. Add the Brussels sprouts to the bowl and toss until they are evenly coated with the olive oil mixture.
5. Transfer the Brussels sprouts to the prepared baking sheet and spread them out in a single layer.
6. Roast in the preheated oven for 15-20 minutes, or until the Brussels sprouts are tender and nicely browned, stirring once halfway through.
7. Remove from the oven and let the roasted Brussels sprouts cool slightly.
8. Garnish with fresh parsley.
9. Serve the lemon garlic roasted Brussels sprouts as a delicious and nutritious keto Mediterranean side dish.

Nutritional Information (per serving): Calories: 110 Protein: 4g Carbohydrates: 12g Fat: 6g Fiber: 5g Cholesterol: 0mg Sodium: 320mg Potassium: 600mg

Mediterranean Cucumber Cups with Tuna Salad

Yield: 4 servings | **Prep time:** 15 minutes | **Cook time:** 0 minutes

Ingredients:

- 2 large cucumbers
- 2 cans (5 ounces each) tuna, drained
- 1/4 cup diced red onion
- 1/4 cup diced tomato
- 1/4 cup diced cucumber
- Salt and pepper, to taste
- 2 tbsp chopped Kalamata olives
- 2 tbsp chopped fresh parsley
- 2 tbsp extra virgin olive oil
- 1 tbsp lemon juice
- 1/2 tsp dried oregano

Directions:

1. Slice the cucumbers and hollow out the centers to create cups.
2. Mix drained tuna, red onion, tomato, cucumber, olives, parsley, olive oil, lemon juice, dried oregano, salt, and pepper in a bowl.
3. Fill each cucumber cup with the tuna salad mixture.
4. Arrange on a serving platter.
5. Serve and enjoy!

Nutritional Information (per serving): Calories: 180 Protein: 21g Carbohydrates: 4g Fat: 9g Fiber: 1g Cholesterol: 25mg Sodium: 430mg Potassium: 410mg

Feta-Stuffed Bacon-Wrapped Dates

Yield: 4 servings | **Prep time:** 10 minutes | **Cook time:** 15 minutes

Ingredients:

- 12 large Medjool dates, pitted
- cubes
- 6 slices of bacon, cut in half
- 4 ounces feta cheese, cut into small

Directions:

1. Preheat the oven to 400°F (200°C) and line a baking sheet with parchment paper.
2. Take each pitted date and stuff it with a cube of feta cheese.
3. Wrap each stuffed date with a half slice of bacon, securing it with a toothpick if needed.
4. Place the bacon-wrapped dates on the prepared baking sheet.
5. Bake in the preheated oven for about 15 minutes, or until the bacon is crispy and cooked through.
6. Remove from the oven and let cool slightly before serving.

Nutritional Information (per serving): Calories: 190 Protein: 6g Carbohydrates: 25g Fat: 8g Fiber: 3g Cholesterol: 22mg Sodium: 280mg Potassium: 420mg

Artichoke and Spinach Dip

Yield: 4 servings | **Prep time:** 10 minutes | **Cook time:** 20 minutes

Ingredients:

- 8 ounces cream cheese, softened
- 1/2 cup mayonnaise
- 1/4 cup grated Parmesan cheese
- 1/4 cup grated mozzarella cheese
- 1 clove garlic, minced
- 1/2 teaspoon dried basil
- canned artichoke hearts, drained
- Salt and pepper to taste
- 1/2 teaspoon dried oregano
- 1/2 teaspoon dried thyme
- 1/2 cup chopped frozen spinach, thawed and drained
- 1/2 cup chopped

Directions:

1. Preheat the oven to 350°F (175°C).
2. In a mixing bowl, combine the softened cream cheese, mayonnaise, Parmesan cheese, mozzarella cheese, minced garlic, dried basil, dried oregano, and dried thyme. Mix well.
3. Add the chopped spinach and artichoke hearts to the mixture. Stir until well combined.
4. Season with salt and pepper to taste.
5. Transfer the mixture to an oven-safe dish and smooth the top.
6. Bake in the preheated oven for 20 minutes, or until the top is golden and bubbly.
7. Remove from the oven and let it cool for a few minutes before serving.

Nutritional Information (per serving): Calories: 270 Protein: 7g Carbohydrates: 5g Fat: 25g Fiber: 2g Cholesterol: 60mg Sodium: 480mg Potassium: 150mg

Marinated Greek Olives

Yield: 4 servings | **Prep time:** 10 minutes | **Cook time:** 0 minutes

Ingredients:

- 2 cups mixed Greek olives (Kalamata, green, black, etc.)
- 2 tablespoons extra virgin olive oil
- 2 cloves garlic, minced
- Freshly ground black pepper, to taste
- 1 teaspoon dried oregano
- 1 teaspoon lemon zest
- 1/4 teaspoon red pepper flakes (optional)

Directions:

1. Rinse the olives under cold water and drain well.
2. In a mixing bowl, combine the olives, extra virgin olive oil, minced garlic, dried oregano, lemon zest, red pepper flakes (if using), and black pepper. Mix well to coat the olives evenly.
3. Cover the bowl and let the olives marinate at room temperature for at least 30 minutes, or refrigerate for a few hours to enhance the flavors.
4. Serve the marinated olives as a snack or as part of a Mediterranean antipasto platter.

Nutritional Information (per serving): Calories: 110 Protein: 0.5g Carbohydrates: 3g Fat: 11g Fiber: 2g Cholesterol: 0mg Sodium: 650mg Potassium: 30mg

Smoked Salmon Cucumber Roll-Ups

Yield: 4 servings | **Prep time:** 15 minutes | **Cook time:** 0 minutes

Ingredients:

- 2 large cucumbers
- 4 ounces smoked salmon
- 4 ounces cream cheese, softened
- Salt and pepper, to taste
- 2 tablespoons fresh dill, chopped
- 1 tablespoon lemon juice

Directions:

1. Slice the cucumbers lengthwise into thin strips using a vegetable peeler or a mandoline slicer.
2. In a small bowl, combine the softened cream cheese, fresh dill, lemon juice, salt, and pepper. Mix well to incorporate all the ingredients.
3. Lay the cucumber slices flat on a clean surface and spread a thin layer of the cream cheese mixture onto each slice.
4. Place a piece of smoked salmon at one end of each cucumber slice and roll it up tightly.
5. Secure the roll-ups with toothpicks if necessary.
6. Repeat the process with the remaining cucumber slices, cream cheese mixture, and smoked salmon.
7. Serve the smoked salmon cucumber roll-ups as an appetizer or snack.

Nutritional Information (per serving): Calories: 90 Protein: 7g Carbohydrates: 3g Fat: 5g Fiber: 1g Cholesterol: 20mg Sodium: 240mg Potassium: 220mg

Baked Parmesan Zucchini Chips

Yield: 4 servings | **Prep time:** 15 minutes | **Cook time:** 15 minutes

Ingredients:

- 2 medium zucchini
- 1/4 cup grated Parmesan cheese
- 1/4 cup almond flour
- 1/2 teaspoon garlic powder
- 1 large egg, beaten
- 1/2 teaspoon dried oregano
- 1/4 teaspoon salt
- 1/4 teaspoon black pepper

Directions:

1. Preheat the oven to 425°F (220°C). Line a baking sheet with parchment paper or lightly grease it.
2. Slice the zucchini into thin rounds, about 1/4-inch thick.
3. In a shallow bowl, combine the grated Parmesan cheese, almond flour, garlic powder, dried oregano, salt, and black pepper.
4. Dip each zucchini slice into the beaten egg, then dredge it in the Parmesan mixture, pressing lightly to adhere.
5. Place the coated zucchini slices on the prepared baking sheet in a single layer.
6. Bake for 12-15 minutes, or until the zucchini chips are golden brown and crispy.
7. Remove from the oven and let cool for a few minutes before serving.

Nutritional Information (per serving): Calories: 90 Protein: 6g Carbohydrates: 5g Fat: 6g Fiber: 2g Cholesterol: 60mg Sodium: 240mg Potassium: 310mg

Greek Yogurt and Cucumber Dip (Tzatziki)

Yield: 4 servings | **Prep time:** 10 minutes | **Cook time:** 0 minutes

Ingredients:

- 1 cup Greek yogurt
- 1/2 cucumber, grated and drained
- 2 cloves garlic, minced
- Salt and pepper, to taste
- 1 tablespoon fresh lemon juice
- 1 tablespoon chopped fresh dill
- 1 tablespoon extra virgin olive oil

Directions:

1. In a medium bowl, combine the Greek yogurt, grated and drained cucumber, minced garlic, lemon juice, fresh dill, and extra virgin olive oil.
2. Stir well to combine all the ingredients.
3. Season with salt and pepper to taste. Adjust the seasoning according to your preference.
4. Cover the bowl and refrigerate the tzatziki for at least 1 hour to allow the flavors to meld together.
5. Serve chilled as a dip with fresh vegetables, grilled meats, or as a spread for wraps and sandwiches.

Nutritional Information (per serving): Calories: 70 Protein: 8g Carbohydrates: 3g Fat: 3g Fiber: 0g Cholesterol: 5mg Sodium: 30mg Potassium: 140mg

Stuffed Avocado with Shrimp Salad

Yield: 2 servings | **Prep time:** 15 minutes | **Cook time:** 0 minutes

Ingredients:

- 2 avocados
- 8 ounces cooked shrimp, peeled and deveined
- 1/4 cup diced cucumber
- 1/4 cup diced red bell pepper
- Salt and pepper, to taste
- 2 tablespoons diced red onion
- 2 tablespoons chopped fresh parsley
- 2 tablespoons mayonnaise
- 1 tablespoon lemon juice

Directions:

1. Cut the avocados in half lengthwise and remove the pits. Scoop out a small amount of flesh from each avocado half to create a larger hollow for the filling.
2. In a bowl, combine the cooked shrimp, diced cucumber, diced red bell pepper, diced red onion, chopped fresh parsley, mayonnaise, and lemon juice. Mix well to coat the ingredients with the dressing.
3. Season the shrimp salad with salt and pepper to taste. Adjust the seasoning according to your preference.
4. Spoon the shrimp salad mixture into the hollowed-out avocados, dividing it evenly among them.
5. Serve the stuffed avocados as a refreshing and satisfying salad or light meal.

Nutritional Information (per serving): Calories: 320 Protein: 16g Carbohydrates: 12g Fat: 25g Fiber: 9g Cholesterol: 125mg Sodium: 380mg Potassium: 850mg

Tomato and Mozzarella Skewers with Basil Pesto

Yield: 4 servings | **Prep time:** 15 minutes | **Cook time:** 0 minutes

Ingredients:

- 16 cherry tomatoes
- 8 small fresh mozzarella balls
- 1/4 cup basil pesto
- Fresh basil leaves

Directions:

1. Thread a cherry tomato onto a skewer, followed by a fresh mozzarella ball and a fresh basil leaf. Repeat this pattern until the skewer is filled, leaving a small space at the end for easy handling.
2. Repeat the process with the remaining skewers and ingredients.
3. Once all the skewers are assembled, drizzle the basil pesto over the tomato and mozzarella skewers.
4. Serve the skewers as a delicious and visually appealing appetizer or snack.

Nutritional Information (per serving): Calories: 160 Protein: 8g Carbohydrates: 3g Fat: 13g Fiber: 1g Cholesterol: 25mg Sodium: 220mg Potassium: 150mg

Meat (Beaf, Pork, Lamb, etc.)

Lemon Herb Roasted Pork Tenderloin

Yield: 4 servings | **Prep time:** 10 minutes | **Cook time:** 25 minutes

Ingredients:

- 1 ½ pounds pork tenderloin
- 2 tablespoons extra virgin olive oil
- 2 cloves garlic, minced
- 1 teaspoon dried thyme
- Salt and black pepper, to taste
- 1 teaspoon dried rosemary
- Zest of 1 lemon
- Juice of 1 lemon

Directions:

1. Preheat the oven to 425°F (220°C). In a small bowl, combine the olive oil, minced garlic, dried thyme, dried rosemary, lemon zest, lemon juice, salt, and black pepper. Mix well.
2. Place the pork tenderloin in a baking dish or on a lined baking sheet.
3. Brush the tenderloin with the prepared herb and lemon mixture, ensuring it is evenly coated.
4. Roast the pork tenderloin in the preheated oven for about 20-25 minutes, or until it reaches an internal temperature of 145°F (63°C).
5. Remove the pork from the oven and let it rest for a few minutes before slicing.
6. Slice the roasted pork tenderloin into medallions and serve.

Nutritional Information: (per serving): Calories: 250 Protein: 36g Carbohydrates: 0g Fat: 10g Fiber: 0g Cholesterol: 110mg Sodium: 320mg Potassium: 560mg

Greek-style Stuffed Pork Tenderloin

Yield: 4 servings | **Prep time:** 15 minutes | **Cook time:** 25 minutes

Ingredients:

- 1 lb pork tenderloin
- 1/4 cup crumbled feta cheese
- 1/4 cup chopped Kalamata olives
- 2 tbsp chopped sun-dried tomatoes
- 1 tbsp olive oil
- 2 cloves garlic, minced
- 1 tsp dried oregano
- Salt and black pepper, to taste

Directions:

1. Preheat oven to 400°F (200°C). Slice pork tenderloin lengthwise without cutting through.
2. Mix feta cheese, olives, sun-dried tomatoes, garlic, oregano, salt, and pepper.
3. Stuff mixture into pork pocket. Secure opening with toothpicks. Sear pork in olive oil over medium-high heat. Transfer skillet to oven and bake for 15-20 minutes. Rest pork before slicing into medallions.
4. Remove toothpicks and serve hot.

Nutritional Information: (per serving): Calories: 260 Protein: 30g Carbohydrates: 4g Fat: 14g Fiber: 1g Cholesterol: 85mg Sodium: 490mg Potassium: 620mg

Moroccan Spiced Ground Beef Stuffed Bell Peppers

Yield: 4 servings | **Prep time:** 15 minutes | **Cook time:** 40 minutes

Ingredients:

- 4 large bell peppers (any color)
- 1 pound ground beef
- 1 small onion, finely chopped
- 2 cloves garlic, minced
- 1 teaspoon ground cumin
- 1 teaspoon ground coriander
- 1/4 cup chopped fresh parsley or cilantro (for garnish)
- 1 teaspoon paprika
- 1/2 teaspoon ground cinnamon
- 1/4 teaspoon cayenne pepper (optional, for added spice)
- Salt and black pepper, to taste
- 1 can (14 ounces) diced tomatoes, drained

Directions:

1. Preheat the oven to 375°F (190°C). Cut off tops of bell peppers and remove seeds and membranes.
2. Cook ground beef in a skillet until browned. Drain any excess fat.
3. Add onion, garlic, cumin, coriander, paprika, cinnamon, cayenne pepper (if using), salt, and black pepper to the skillet. Cook for 1 minute. Stir in drained diced tomatoes.
4. Stuff each bell pepper with the ground beef mixture and place in a baking dish.
5. Cover with foil and bake for 25 minutes. Remove foil and bake for an additional 10-15 minutes until peppers are tender. Garnish with fresh parsley or cilantro before serving.

Nutritional Information: (per serving) Calories: 320 Protein: 22g Carbohydrates: 12g Fat: 21g Fiber: 4g Cholesterol: 65mg Sodium: 620mg Potassium: 720mg

Mediterranean Stuffed Bell Peppers

Yield: 4 servings | **Prep time:** 20 minutes | **Cook time:** 30 minutes

Ingredients:

- 4 bell peppers (any color)
- 1 lb ground beef or turkey
- 1 small onion, finely chopped
- 2 cloves garlic, minced
- 1/2 cup chopped tomatoes
- Salt and black pepper, to taste
- 1/4 cup chopped Kalamata olives
- 1/4 cup crumbled feta cheese
- 2 tbsp chopped fresh parsley
- 2 tbsp extra virgin olive oil
- 1 tsp dried oregano

Directions:

1. Preheat oven to 375°F (190°C). In a skillet, sauté onion and garlic in olive oil until softened.
2. Add ground beef or turkey to the skillet and cook until browned. Drain excess fat.
3. Stir in tomatoes, Kalamata olives, dried oregano, salt, and black pepper. Cook for 2-3 minutes.
4. Remove from heat and mix in crumbled feta cheese and fresh parsley. Stuff bell peppers with the meat mixture and place in a baking dish. Bake for 25-30 minutes until peppers are tender and filling is heated through.

Nutritional Information: (per serving) Calories: 290 Protein: 21g Carbohydrates: 12g Fat: 18g Fiber: 4g Cholesterol: 65mg Sodium: 640mg Potassium: 750mg

Moroccan Spiced Beef Kabobs

Yield: 4 servings | **Prep time:** 20 minutes | **Cook time:** 12 minutes

Ingredients:

- 1.5 lbs beef sirloin, cut into cubes
- 1 onion, cut into chunks
- 1 bell pepper, cut into chunks
- 8 cherry tomatoes
- 2 tbsp olive oil
- 2 tbsp lemon juice
- 2 cloves garlic, minced
- Wooden skewers, soaked in water
- 1 tsp ground cumin
- 1 tsp ground coriander
- 1/2 tsp paprika
- 1/2 tsp ground turmeric
- 1/4 tsp ground cinnamon
- Salt and black pepper, to taste

Directions:

1. In a bowl, combine olive oil, lemon juice, minced garlic, ground cumin, ground coriander, paprika, ground turmeric, ground cinnamon, salt, and black pepper.
2. Add beef cubes to the bowl and toss to coat them evenly with the spice mixture. Let marinate for at least 15 minutes. Preheat the grill or grill pan over medium-high heat.
3. Thread the marinated beef cubes onto the soaked wooden skewers, alternating with onion, bell pepper, and cherry tomatoes.
4. Grill the beef kabobs for about 10-12 minutes, turning occasionally, until cooked to desired doneness.
5. Serve the Moroccan spiced beef kabobs hot.

Nutritional Information: (per serving) Calories: 330 Protein: 32g Carbohydrates: 7g Fat: 19g Fiber: 2g Cholesterol: 95mg Sodium: 410mg Potassium: 660mg

Greek Lemon Chicken Thighs

Yield: 4 servings | **Prep time:** 10 minutes | **Cook time:** 30 minutes

Ingredients:

- 4 bone-in, skin-on chicken thighs
- 1 lemon, juiced and zested
- 2 cloves garlic, minced
- 2 tbsp extra virgin olive oil
- Fresh parsley, chopped (for garnish)
- 1 tsp dried oregano
- 1/2 tsp dried thyme
- Salt and black pepper, to taste

Directions:

1. Preheat oven to 400°F (200°C).
2. In a bowl, combine lemon juice, lemon zest, minced garlic, olive oil, dried oregano, dried thyme, salt, and black pepper. Place chicken thighs in a baking dish and pour the lemon mixture over them.
3. Bake for 25-30 minutes until chicken is cooked through and skin is crispy.
4. Remove from oven and let rest for a few minutes. Serve hot, garnished with fresh parsley.

Nutritional Information: (per serving) Calories: 380 Protein: 33g Carbohydrates: 3g Fat: 26g Fiber: 1g Cholesterol: 175mg Sodium: 550mg Potassium: 410mg

Herb-Roasted Pork Tenderloin

Yield: 4 servings | **Prep time:** 10 minutes | **Cook time:** 25 minutes

Ingredients:

- 1.5 lbs pork tenderloin
- 2 tbsp olive oil
- 2 cloves garlic, minced
- Salt and black pepper, to taste
- 1 tsp dried rosemary
- 1 tsp dried thyme
- 1/2 tsp dried oregano

Directions:

1. Preheat the oven to 400°F (200°C). In a small bowl, mix together olive oil, minced garlic, dried rosemary, dried thyme, dried oregano, salt, and black pepper.
2. Rub the herb mixture all over the pork tenderloin, ensuring it's evenly coated.
3. Place the pork tenderloin on a baking sheet or in a roasting pan.
4. Roast in the preheated oven for about 20-25 minutes, or until the internal temperature reaches 145°F (63°C) for medium doneness.
5. Remove from the oven and let the pork rest for a few minutes before slicing.
6. Slice the herb-roasted pork tenderloin and serve.

Nutritional Information: (per serving) Calories: 240 Protein: 34g Carbohydrates: 1g Fat: 10g Fiber: 0g Cholesterol: 105mg Sodium: 310mg Potassium: 580mg

Grilled Tandoori Chicken Skewers

Yield: 4 servings | **Prep time:** 15 minutes | **Cook time:** 15 minutes

Ingredients:

- 1.5 lbs boneless, skinless chicken breasts, cut into cubes
- 1/2 cup plain Greek yogurt
- 2 tbsp lemon juice
- 2 cloves garlic, minced
- 1 tbsp grated ginger
- Fresh cilantro, chopped (for garnish)
- 1 tbsp ground cumin
- 1 tbsp ground coriander
- 1 tsp ground turmeric
- 1/2 tsp paprika
- 1/2 tsp cayenne pepper (optional)
- Salt and black pepper, to taste

Directions:

1. In a bowl, combine Greek yogurt, lemon juice, minced garlic, grated ginger, cumin, coriander, turmeric, paprika, cayenne pepper (if desired), salt, and black pepper.
2. Add chicken cubes to the marinade and mix well. Marinate for at least 1 hour.
3. Preheat grill to medium-high heat. Thread chicken cubes onto skewers.
4. Grill skewers for 12-15 minutes, turning occasionally, until cooked through and slightly charred.
5. Remove from grill and let rest. Garnish with fresh cilantro and serve hot.

Nutritional Information: (per serving) Calories: 250 Protein: 38g Carbohydrates: 6g Fat: 6g Fiber: 1g Cholesterol: 95mg Sodium: 480mg Potassium: 590mg

Rosemary Garlic Roast Beef

Yield: 4 servings | **Prep time:** 10 minutes | **Cook time:** 60 minutes

Ingredients:

- 2 lbs beef roast (such as sirloin or tenderloin)
- 4 cloves garlic, minced
- Salt and black pepper, to taste
- 2 tbsp fresh rosemary, chopped
- 2 tbsp olive oil

Directions:

1. Preheat the oven to 350°F (175°C).
2. In a small bowl, combine minced garlic, chopped rosemary, olive oil, salt, and black pepper.
3. Rub the mixture all over the beef roast, ensuring it is evenly coated.
4. Place the roast on a rack in a roasting pan.
5. Roast the beef in the preheated oven, calculating the cooking time based on the weight of the roast (about 20 minutes per pound for medium-rare).
6. Check the internal temperature of the roast using a meat thermometer. For medium-rare, the thermometer should read 135°F (57°C).
7. Once cooked to the desired level of doneness, remove the roast from the oven and let it rest for 10-15 minutes before slicing. Slice the roast beef into thin slices and serve.

Nutritional Information: (per serving) Calories: 350 Protein: 48g Carbohydrates: 0g Fat: 17g Fiber: 0g Cholesterol: 130mg Sodium: 600mg Potassium: 720mg

Lamb Kofta with Yogurt Sauce

Yield: 4 servings | **Prep time:** 20 minutes | **Cook time:** 15 minutes

Ingredients:

- 1 pound ground lamb
- 1/2 cup finely chopped red onion
- 2 cloves garlic, minced
- 1/4 cup finely chopped fresh parsley
- 1/4 cup finely chopped fresh mint
- 2 tablespoons olive oil
- 1 teaspoon ground cumin
- 1 teaspoon ground coriander
- 1/2 teaspoon ground cinnamon
- 1/2 teaspoon salt
- 1/4 teaspoon black pepper

Directions:

1. In a large bowl, combine the ground lamb, red onion, garlic, parsley, mint, cumin, coriander, cinnamon, salt, and black pepper. Mix well to combine all the ingredients.
2. Shape the lamb mixture into small oblong patties, about 2 inches long and 1 inch wide.
3. Heat the olive oil in a large skillet over medium heat. Cook the lamb kofta for about 5-7 minutes per side until browned and cooked through.
4. While the kofta are cooking, prepare the yogurt sauce. In a small bowl, combine the Greek yogurt, lemon juice, mint, salt, and pepper. Stir well to combine. Serve the lamb kofta hot with the yogurt sauce on the side.

Nutritional Information: (per serving) Calories: 320 Protein: 26g Carbohydrates: 5g Fat: 22g Fiber: 1g Cholesterol: 90mg Sodium: 420mg Potassium: 450mg

Balsamic Glazed Pork Loin

Yield: 4 servings | **Prep time:** 10 minutes | **Cook time:** 40 minutes

Ingredients:

- 1.5 pounds pork loin
- 1/4 cup balsamic vinegar
- 2 tablespoons olive oil
- 2 cloves garlic, minced
- 1/4 teaspoon black pepper
- 1 tablespoon Dijon mustard
- 1 tablespoon fresh rosemary, chopped
- 1 teaspoon dried thyme
- 1/2 teaspoon salt

Directions:

1. Preheat the oven to 375°F (190°C).
2. In a small bowl, whisk together the balsamic vinegar, olive oil, minced garlic, Dijon mustard, chopped rosemary, dried thyme, salt, and black pepper to make the glaze.
3. Place the pork loin in a baking dish and pour the glaze over it, reserving a small amount for basting later.
4. Rub the glaze all over the pork loin, ensuring it is coated evenly.
5. Roast the pork loin in the preheated oven for about 35-40 minutes, or until the internal temperature reaches 145°F (63°C) using a meat thermometer.
6. While the pork is cooking, baste it with the reserved glaze every 10-15 minutes to enhance the flavor and create a shiny glaze. Remove the pork loin from the oven and let it rest for 5-10 minutes before slicing.
7. Slice the pork loin into medallions and serve hot.

Nutritional Information: (per serving) Calories: 280 Protein: 35g Carbohydrates: 3g Fat: 13g Fiber: 0g Cholesterol: 105mg Sodium: 370mg Potassium: 560mg

Spicy Lamb Lettuce Wraps

Yield: 4 servings | **Prep time:** 15 minutes | **Cook time:** 10 minutes

Ingredients:

- 1 lb ground lamb
- 2 tbsp olive oil
- 2 cloves garlic, minced
- 1 small onion, diced
- 1 red bell pepper, diced
- 2 tsp ground cumin
- 1 tsp ground coriander
- 1/2 tsp paprika
- 1/2 tsp cayenne pepper (adjust to taste)
- Salt and black pepper, to taste
- 8 large lettuce leaves
- Optional toppings: diced tomatoes, diced cucumbers, mint, tzatziki sauce

Directions:

1. Heat olive oil in a skillet over medium heat. Sauté garlic, onion, and bell pepper until softened.
2. Add ground lamb and cook until browned.
3. Stir in cumin, coriander, paprika, cayenne pepper, salt, and black pepper. Cook for 2-3 minutes.
4. Spoon lamb mixture onto lettuce leaves. Top with optional toppings.
5. Roll up lettuce leaves to create wraps. Serve as a flavorful meal.

Nutritional Information: (per serving) Calories: 365 Protein: 21g Carbohydrates: 7g Fat: 29g Fiber: 2g Cholesterol: 84mg Sodium: 138mg Potassium: 464mg

Mediterranean Stuffed Cabbage Rolls

Yield: 4 servings | **Prep time:** 30 minutes | **Cook time:** 45 minutes

Ingredients:

- 8 large cabbage leaves
- 1 lb ground beef
- 1/4 cup diced onion
- 2 cloves garlic, minced
- 1/2 cup cauliflower rice
- 1/4 cup chopped parsley
- 1 tsp dried oregano
- Optional garnish: chopped parsley
- 1/2 tsp ground cumin
- 1/2 tsp paprika
- 1/4 tsp cinnamon
- Salt and black pepper, to taste
- 1 cup sugar-free marinara sauce
- 1/2 cup chicken broth

Directions:

1. Blanch cabbage leaves in boiling water for 2 minutes and set aside.
2. Cook ground beef, onion, and garlic until browned. Drain fat.
3. Add cauliflower rice, parsley, tomato paste, oregano, cumin, salt, and pepper. Cook for 5 minutes.
4. Preheat oven to 375°F (190°C).
5. Fill cabbage leaves with beef mixture, roll tightly, and place in a baking dish.
6. Pour marinara sauce over rolls.
7. Cover with foil and bake for 30 minutes.
8. Remove foil, sprinkle with feta cheese, and bake for 10 more minutes.
9. Garnish with parsley and serve.

Nutritional Information: (per serving) Calories: 285 Protein: 21g Carbohydrates: 8g Fat: 19g Fiber: 3g Cholesterol: 63mg Sodium: 483mg Potassium: 554mg

Garlic Butter Steak with Roasted Vegetables

Yield: 4 servings | **Prep time:** 15 minutes | **Cook time:** 25 minutes

Ingredients:

- 1.5 lbs steak
- 4 cloves garlic, minced
- 2 tbsp butter, melted
- 1 tsp dried thyme
- 1/2 tsp garlic powder
- Salt and black pepper
- 1 lb mixed vegetables
- 2 tbsp olive oil
- 1 tsp dried rosemary

Directions:

1. Preheat oven to 425°F (220°C). Mix minced garlic, melted butter, dried thyme, salt, and black pepper.
2. Brush garlic butter mixture on both sides of the steak. Sear steak in a skillet over medium-high heat for 2-3 minutes per side. Transfer skillet to oven and cook steak for 10-15 minutes.
3. Toss mixed vegetables with olive oil, dried rosemary, garlic powder, salt, and black pepper.
4. Roast vegetables in the oven for 15-20 minutes.
5. Slice steak against the grain. Serve garlic butter steak with roasted vegetables.

Nutritional Information: (per serving) Calories: 380 Protein: 30g Carbohydrates: 10g Fat: 25g Fiber: 4g Cholesterol: 95mg Sodium: 220mg Potassium: 810mg

Grilled Moroccan Spiced Lamb Chops

Yield: 4 servings | **Prep time:** 10 minutes | **Cook time:** 12 minutes

Ingredients:

- 8 lamb chops
- 2 tablespoons olive oil
- 2 teaspoons ground cumin
- 2 teaspoons ground coriander
- 1 teaspoon ground paprika
- Fresh mint leaves, for garnish (optional)
- 1/2 teaspoon ground cinnamon
- 1/2 teaspoon ground ginger
- 1/2 teaspoon salt
- 1/4 teaspoon black pepper

Directions:

1. Preheat the grill to medium-high heat.
2. In a small bowl, combine the olive oil, ground cumin, ground coriander, ground paprika, ground cinnamon, ground ginger, salt, and black pepper to make the spice rub.
3. Pat the lamb chops dry with paper towels and brush them with the spice rub on both sides, pressing gently to adhere the spices.
4. Place the lamb chops on the preheated grill and cook for about 5-6 minutes per side for medium-rare doneness. Adjust the cooking time according to your desired level of doneness.
5. Remove the lamb chops from the grill and let them rest for a few minutes before serving.
6. Optional: Garnish with fresh mint leaves for added freshness and flavor.
7. Serve the grilled Moroccan spiced lamb chops hot.

Nutritional Information: (per serving) Calories: 340 Protein: 32g Carbohydrates: 1g Fat: 23g Fiber: 0g Cholesterol: 110mg Sodium: 350mg Potassium: 400mg

Poultry

Greek Lemon Chicken with Olives

Yield: 4 servings | **Prep time:** 15 minutes | **Cook time:** 30 minutes

Ingredients:

- 4 bone-in, skin-on chicken thighs
- 2 tablespoons olive oil
- 4 cloves garlic, minced
- 1 tablespoon dried oregano
- Fresh parsley, for garnish
- 1 teaspoon dried thyme
- 1 lemon, zest and juice
- 1/2 cup pitted Kalamata olives
- Salt and pepper, to taste

Directions:

1. Preheat the oven to 375°F (190°C). In a small bowl, mix together the olive oil, minced garlic, dried oregano, dried thyme, lemon zest, and lemon juice.
2. Place the chicken thighs in a baking dish and season them with salt and pepper.
3. Pour the olive oil mixture over the chicken thighs, making sure they are well coated.
4. Scatter the Kalamata olives around the chicken in the baking dish.
5. Bake in the preheated oven for about 25-30 minutes, or until the chicken is cooked through and the skin is crispy. Remove from the oven and let the chicken rest for a few minutes before serving.
6. Garnish with fresh parsley and serve with your favorite low-carb Mediterranean side dish.

Nutritional Information: (per serving) Calories: 300 Protein: 27g Carbohydrates: 6g Fat: 18g Fiber: 2g Cholesterol: 75mg Sodium: 800mg Potassium: 400mg

Moroccan Spiced Chicken Skewers

Yield: 4 servings | **Prep time:** 15 minutes | **Cook time:** 15 minutes

Ingredients:

- 1.5 pounds boneless, skinless chicken breasts, cut into 1-inch cubes
- 2 tablespoons olive oil
- 2 tablespoons lemon juice
- 2 teaspoons ground cumin
- 1 teaspoon ground paprika
- 1 tablespoon fresh cilantro, chopped (optional, for garnish)
- 1 teaspoon ground coriander
- 1/2 teaspoon ground cinnamon
- 1/2 teaspoon ground turmeric
- 1/2 teaspoon sea salt
- 1/4 teaspoon black pepper
- 2 cloves garlic, minced

Directions:

1. Preheat the grill or grill pan over medium-high heat.
2. In a mixing bowl, combine olive oil, lemon juice, cumin, paprika, coriander, cinnamon, turmeric, salt, pepper, and garlic.
3. Add chicken cubes to the marinade and toss to coat. Thread chicken onto skewers.
4. Grill skewers for 6-8 minutes on each side until cooked through and grill marks appear.
5. Let skewers rest for a few minutes.
6. Serve garnished with fresh cilantro, if desired.

Nutritional Information: (per serving) Calories: 280 Protein: 36g Carbohydrates: 2g Fat: 14g Fiber: 1g Cholesterol: 95mg Sodium: 450mg Potassium: 550mg

Italian Herb Roasted Chicken Thighs

Yield: 4 servings | **Prep time:** 10 minutes | **Cook time:** 30 minutes

Ingredients:

- 8 bone-in, skin-on chicken thighs
- 2 tablespoons olive oil
- 2 teaspoons dried oregano
- 1 teaspoon dried basil
- 1 teaspoon dried thyme
- Fresh basil leaves, for garnish (optional)
- 1 teaspoon garlic powder
- 1 teaspoon onion powder
- 1/2 teaspoon sea salt
- 1/4 teaspoon black pepper

Directions:

1. Preheat the oven to 425°F (220°C). Place the chicken thighs on a baking sheet lined with parchment paper.
2. In a small bowl, combine olive oil, dried oregano, dried basil, dried thyme, garlic powder, onion powder, sea salt, and black pepper. Mix well to create an herb rub.
3. Rub the herb mixture evenly over both sides of the chicken thighs, making sure they are well coated.
4. Arrange the chicken thighs in a single layer on the baking sheet.
5. Place the baking sheet in the preheated oven and roast for about 25-30 minutes, or until the chicken is golden brown and cooked through, with an internal temperature of 165°F (74°C).
6. Remove the chicken thighs from the oven and let them rest for a few minutes before serving.
7. Garnish with fresh basil leaves, if desired.

Nutritional Information: (per serving) Calories: 330 Protein: 28g Carbohydrates: 0g Fat: 23g Fiber: 0g Cholesterol: 150mg Sodium: 380mg Potassium: 300mg

Keto Greek Chicken Salad

Yield: 4 servings | **Prep time:** 15 minutes | **Cook time:** 20 minutes

Ingredients:

- 2 boneless, skinless chicken breasts
- 2 tbsp olive oil
- 1 tbsp lemon juice
- 1 tsp dried oregano
- 1/2 tsp garlic powder
- 1/2 tsp sea salt
- 1/4 tsp black pepper
- 4 cups mixed salad greens
- Salt and pepper, to taste (for dressing)
- 1 cup diced cucumber
- 1 cup halved cherry tomatoes
- 1/4 cup thinly sliced red onion
- 1/4 cup pitted and halved Kalamata olives
- 1/4 cup crumbled feta cheese
- 2 tbsp extra-virgin olive oil (for dressing)
- 1 tbsp red wine vinegar (for dressing)
- 1/2 tsp dried oregano (for dressing)

Directions:

1. Grill chicken breasts over medium-high heat for 8-10 minutes per side. Let them rest and slice into strips.
2. In a salad bowl, combine greens, cucumber, tomatoes, red onion, olives, and feta cheese.
3. Whisk together extra-virgin olive oil, red wine vinegar, dried oregano, salt, and pepper to make the dressing.
4. Drizzle the dressing over the salad and toss to coat. Divide onto plates and top with sliced grilled chicken.

Nutritional Information: (per serving) Calories: 280 Protein: 25g Carbohydrates: 7g Fat: 17g Fiber: 2g Cholesterol: 65mg Sodium: 400mg Potassium: 550mg

Lemon Herb Grilled Chicken Breast

Yield: 4 servings | **Prep time:** 10 minutes | **Cook time:** 12 minutes

Ingredients:

- 4 boneless, skinless chicken breasts
- 2 tbsp olive oil
- 2 tbsp lemon juice
- 1 tbsp chopped fresh parsley
- 1 tbsp chopped fresh thyme
- 1/4 tsp black pepper
- 1 tsp grated lemon zest
- 1/2 tsp dried oregano
- 1/2 tsp garlic powder
- 1/2 tsp sea salt

Directions:

1. Preheat the grill to medium-high heat.
2. In a small bowl, whisk together olive oil, lemon juice, parsley, thyme, lemon zest, oregano, garlic powder, sea salt, and black pepper to make the marinade.
3. Place chicken breasts in a shallow dish and pour the marinade over them. Let them marinate for at least 10 minutes. Remove the chicken from the marinade and discard the excess.
4. Grill the chicken breasts for about 6 minutes per side until cooked through.
5. Let the chicken rest for a few minutes before serving. Serve with a squeeze of fresh lemon juice, if desired.

Nutritional Information: (per serving) Calories: 250 Protein: 38g Carbohydrates: 1g Fat: 10g Fiber: 0g Cholesterol: 100mg Sodium: 300mg Potassium: 450mg

Oven-Baked Mediterranean Chicken Thighs

Yield: 4 servings | **Prep time:** 10 minutes | **Cook time:** 30 minutes

Ingredients:

- 8 bone-in, skin-on chicken thighs
- 2 tablespoons olive oil
- 2 cloves garlic, minced
- 1 tablespoon lemon juice
- 1 teaspoon dried oregano
- 1 teaspoon dried thyme
- 1/2 teaspoon paprika
- Fresh parsley, for garnish (optional)
- 1/2 teaspoon sea salt
- 1/4 teaspoon black pepper
- 1/4 cup pitted Kalamata olives
- 1/4 cup diced sun-dried tomatoes (packed in oil)
- 1/4 cup crumbled feta cheese

Directions:

1. Preheat the oven to 425°F (220°C). Place the chicken thighs in a baking dish.
2. In a small bowl, combine olive oil, minced garlic, lemon juice, dried oregano, dried thyme, paprika, sea salt, and black pepper. Mix well to create a marinade.
3. Pour the marinade over the chicken thighs, making sure they are well coated.
4. Scatter the Kalamata olives and diced sun-dried tomatoes over the chicken.
5. Bake in the preheated oven for 25-30 minutes, or until the chicken is cooked through and the skin is crispy and golden brown. Remove from the oven and sprinkle crumbled feta cheese over the chicken.
6. Garnish with fresh parsley, if desired, before serving.

Nutritional Information: (per serving) Calories: 380 Protein: 28g Carbohydrates: 4g Fat: 28g Fiber: 1g Cholesterol: 140mg Sodium: 520mg Potassium: 420mg

Greek Chicken Souvlaki with Feta Cheese

Yield: 4 servings | **Prep time:** 15 minutes | **Cook time:** 12 minutes

Ingredients:

- 1.5 lbs boneless, skinless chicken breasts, cubed
- 1/4 cup olive oil
- 2 tbsp lemon juice
- 2 cloves garlic, minced
- 1 tsp dried oregano
- 1 tsp dried thyme
- 1/2 tsp paprika
- Tzatziki sauce, for serving
- 1/2 tsp sea salt
- 1/4 tsp black pepper
- 4 pita bread rounds
- 1 cup diced cucumber
- 1/2 cup diced tomatoes
- 1/4 cup diced red onion
- 1/4 cup crumbled feta cheese

Directions:

1. In a bowl, combine olive oil, lemon juice, minced garlic, dried oregano, dried thyme, paprika, sea salt, and black pepper for the marinade.
2. Toss the chicken cubes in the marinade and let them marinate for 10 minutes.
3. Preheat a grill or grill pan over medium-high heat. Thread the marinated chicken onto skewers and grill for 5-6 minutes per side. Warm the pita bread rounds on the grill for a minute on each side.
4. Remove the chicken skewers from the grill and let them rest.
5. Assemble the souvlaki by placing grilled chicken on a warmed pita bread round. Top with cucumber, tomatoes, red onion, and feta cheese. Drizzle with tzatziki sauce and roll up the pita bread.

Nutritional Information: (per serving) Calories: 400 Protein: 32g Carbohydrates: 24g Fat: 18g Fiber: 3g Cholesterol: 80mg Sodium: 550mg Potassium: 550mg

Lemon Garlic Roasted Chicken Drumsticks

Yield: 4 servings | **Prep time:** 10 minutes | **Cook time:** 35 minutes

Ingredients:

- 8 chicken drumsticks
- 2 tablespoons olive oil
- 2 cloves garlic, minced
- 2 tablespoons lemon juice
- 1 teaspoon lemon zest
- Fresh parsley, for garnish (optional)
- 1 teaspoon dried oregano
- 1/2 teaspoon dried thyme
- 1/2 teaspoon sea salt
- 1/4 teaspoon black pepper

Directions:

1. Preheat oven to 425°F (220°C). In a bowl, mix olive oil, minced garlic, lemon juice, lemon zest, dried oregano, dried thyme, sea salt, and black pepper.
2. Place chicken drumsticks in a baking dish and coat them with the marinade.
3. Arrange drumsticks in a single layer and roast for 30-35 minutes, until chicken is cooked through and the skin is crispy. Let the drumsticks rest for a few minutes before serving.
4. Garnish with fresh parsley, if desired.

Nutritional Information: (per serving) Calories: 300 Protein: 28g Carbohydrates: 1g Fat: 20g Fiber: 0g Cholesterol: 160mg Sodium: 400mg Potassium: 300mg

Mediterranean Chicken and Vegetable Skillet

Yield: 4 servings | **Prep time:** 15 minutes | **Cook time:** 20 minutes

Ingredients:

- 1 lb boneless, skinless chicken breasts, cut into bite-sized pieces
- 2 tbsp olive oil
- 2 cloves garlic, minced
- 1 red bell pepper, sliced
- 1 yellow bell pepper, sliced
- 1 small zucchini, sliced
- Fresh parsley, for garnish (optional)
- 1 small eggplant, diced
- 1 cup cherry tomatoes, halved
- 1 tsp dried oregano
- 1 tsp dried basil
- 1/2 tsp sea salt
- 1/4 tsp black pepper
- 1/4 cup crumbled feta cheese

Directions:

1. Heat 1 tbsp olive oil in a large skillet over medium heat.
2. Cook chicken until browned and cooked through, about 6-8 minutes. Remove and set aside.
3. In the same skillet, heat the remaining 1 tbsp olive oil and sauté minced garlic for 1 minute.
4. Add bell peppers, zucchini, eggplant, cherry tomatoes, dried oregano, dried basil, sea salt, and black pepper. Cook for 8-10 minutes, until vegetables are tender.
5. Return cooked chicken to the skillet and toss to combine.
6. Sprinkle with crumbled feta cheese.
7. Garnish with fresh parsley, if desired.

Nutritional Information: (per serving) Calories: 300 Protein: 30g Carbohydrates: 12g Fat: 14g Fiber: 5g Cholesterol: 80mg Sodium: 450mg Potassium: 900mg

Greek Yogurt Marinated Chicken Wings

Yield: 4 servings | **Prep time:** 10 minutes | **Cook time:** 25 minutes

Ingredients:

- 2 lbs chicken wings
- 1 cup Greek yogurt
- 2 tbsp lemon juice
- 2 cloves garlic, minced
- Fresh parsley, for garnish (optional)
- 1 tbsp dried oregano
- 1 tsp paprika
- 1/2 tsp sea salt
- 1/4 tsp black pepper

Directions:

1. In a bowl, combine Greek yogurt, lemon juice, minced garlic, dried oregano, paprika, sea salt, and black pepper.
2. Toss chicken wings in the marinade, ensuring they are evenly coated. Marinate for at least 30 minutes or refrigerate overnight.
3. Preheat the oven to 425°F (220°C) and line a baking sheet with parchment paper.
4. Arrange the marinated chicken wings on the baking sheet.
5. Bake for 20-25 minutes, flipping halfway through, until golden brown and cooked through.
6. Let the wings cool for a few minutes. Garnish with fresh parsley, if desired.

Nutritional Information: (per serving) Calories: 280 Protein: 25g Carbohydrates: 4g Fat: 18g Fiber: 0g Cholesterol: 100mg Sodium: 300mg Potassium: 250mg

Mediterranean Chicken and Cauliflower Rice Bowl

Yield: 4 servings | **Prep time:** 15 minutes | **Cook time:** 25 minutes

Ingredients:

- 1 lb boneless, skinless chicken breasts, diced
- 2 tbsp olive oil
- 2 cloves garlic, minced
- 1 tsp each dried oregano and dried basil
- 1/2 tsp sea salt
- 1/4 tsp black pepper
- 1 small head cauliflower, riced
- Fresh parsley, for garnish (optional)
- 1 cup cherry tomatoes, halved
- 1/2 cup diced cucumber
- 1/4 cup sliced Kalamata olives
- 2 tbsp finely chopped red onion
- 2 tbsp fresh lemon juice
- 2 tbsp extra-virgin olive oil

Directions:

1. In a skillet, heat 1 tbsp olive oil and sauté garlic. Add chicken and cook until browned and cooked through. Set aside.
2. In the same skillet, add remaining 1 tbsp olive oil and sauté cauliflower rice until tender.
3. In a bowl, combine cherry tomatoes, cucumber, olives, red onion, lemon juice, and extra-virgin olive oil.
4. Divide cauliflower rice among bowls. Top with cooked chicken and tomato-cucumber mixture.
5. Garnish with fresh parsley, if desired.

Nutritional Information: (per serving) Calories: 320 Protein: 30g Carbohydrates: 12g Fat: 18g Fiber: 4g Cholesterol: 75mg Sodium: 500mg Potassium: 900mg

Italian Baked Chicken Parmesan

Yield: 4 servings | **Prep time:** 15 minutes | **Cook time:** 25 minutes

Ingredients:

- 4 boneless, skinless chicken breasts
- 1/2 cup almond flour
- 1/4 cup grated Parmesan cheese
- 1 tsp each dried basil and dried oregano
- Fresh basil leaves, for garnish (optional)
- 1/2 tsp each garlic powder, sea salt, and black pepper
- 1 large egg, beaten
- 1 cup sugar-free marinara sauce
- 1 cup shredded mozzarella cheese

Directions:

1. Preheat oven to 400°F (200°C). Line a baking sheet with parchment paper.
2. In a shallow bowl, combine almond flour, grated Parmesan cheese, dried basil, dried oregano, garlic powder, sea salt, and black pepper.
3. Dip chicken breasts in beaten egg, then coat with almond flour mixture. Place on baking sheet.
4. Bake for 20 minutes, until chicken is cooked and coating is crispy.
5. Remove from oven, spoon marinara sauce over each breast, and top with mozzarella cheese.
6. Return to oven and bake for 5 minutes, until cheese is melted and bubbly.
7. Garnish with fresh basil leaves, if desired.

Nutritional Information: (per serving) Calories: 320 Protein: 38g Carbohydrates: 6g Fat: 14g Fiber: 2g Cholesterol: 150mg Sodium: 700mg Potassium: 600mg

Lemon Herb Grilled Chicken Skewers

Yield: 4 servings | **Prep time:** 15 minutes | **Cook time:** 12 minutes

Ingredients:

- 1.5 lbs boneless, skinless chicken breasts, cubed
- Juice and zest of 2 lemons
- 3 tbsp olive oil
- 2 cloves garlic, minced
- Wooden skewers, soaked in water
- 1 tbsp chopped fresh parsley
- 1 tsp dried oregano
- 1/2 tsp dried thyme
- 1/2 tsp sea salt
- 1/4 tsp black pepper

Directions:

1. In a bowl, combine lemon juice, lemon zest, olive oil, minced garlic, parsley, oregano, thyme, sea salt, and black pepper.
2. Add chicken cubes to the bowl and marinate in the refrigerator for 30 minutes to 4 hours.
3. Preheat grill to medium-high heat.
4. Thread marinated chicken cubes onto soaked wooden skewers.
5. Grill skewers for about 6 minutes per side, until chicken is cooked through and has grill marks.
6. Let skewers rest for a few minutes before serving.

Nutritional Information: (per serving) Calories: 250 Protein: 30g Carbohydrates: 3g Fat: 12g Fiber: 1g Cholesterol: 85mg Sodium: 350mg Potassium: 420mg

Greek Chicken Zoodle Soup

Yield: 4 servings | **Prep time:** 15 minutes | **Cook time:** 25 minutes

Ingredients:

- 1 tbsp olive oil
- 1 onion, diced
- 2 cloves garlic, minced
- 2 carrots, sliced
- 2 celery stalks, sliced
- 4 cups chicken broth
- 1 can diced tomatoes (14 oz)
- Fresh parsley, chopped (for garnish)
- 1 tsp dried oregano
- 1/2 tsp dried thyme
- 1/2 tsp dried rosemary
- Salt and pepper to taste
- 1 lb cooked, shredded chicken breasts
- 2 medium zucchini, spiralized into zoodles
- Juice of 1 lemon

Directions:

1. Heat olive oil in a large pot. Sauté onion and garlic.
2. Add carrots and celery, cook until slightly softened.
3. Pour in chicken broth, diced tomatoes, and spices. Simmer for 15 minutes.
4. Add shredded chicken and simmer for 5 minutes.
5. Add zucchini noodles and cook for 2-3 minutes.
6. Stir in lemon juice. Adjust seasonings if needed.
7. Serve hot, garnished with fresh parsley.

Nutritional Information: (per serving) Calories: 220 Protein: 25g Carbs: 12g Fat: 8g Fiber: 4g Cholesterol: 55mg Sodium: 800mg Potassium: 900mg

Moroccan Chicken Tagine with Olives and Artichokes

Yield: 4 servings | **Prep time:** 15 minutes | **Cook time:** 45 minutes

Ingredients:

- 1.5 lbs bone-in chicken pieces
- 2 tbsp olive oil
- 1 onion, diced
- 3 cloves garlic, minced
- 1 tsp ground cumin
- 1 tsp ground coriander
- 1/2 tsp ground cinnamon
- Fresh cilantro or parsley, chopped (for garnish)
- 1/2 tsp ground turmeric
- 1/4 tsp cayenne pepper (optional)
- Salt and pepper to taste
- 1 cup chicken broth
- 1 can diced tomatoes (14 oz)
- 1 cup green olives, pitted
- 1 cup artichoke hearts, quartered

Directions:

1. Heat olive oil in a large pot or tagine over medium heat.
2. Add chicken pieces and brown them on all sides. Remove and set aside.
3. In the same pot, sauté onion and garlic until softened.
4. Add ground cumin, coriander, cinnamon, turmeric, cayenne pepper (if using), salt, and pepper. Stir well to coat the onions and garlic.
5. Pour in chicken broth and diced tomatoes. Bring to a simmer.
6. Return the chicken to the pot, cover, and cook over low heat for 30 minutes.
7. Add green olives and artichoke hearts. Continue cooking for another 10-15 minutes, until the chicken is tender and cooked through.
8. Adjust the seasoning if needed.
9. Serve hot, garnished with fresh cilantro or parsley.

Nutritional Information: (per serving) Calories: 350 Protein: 28g Carbohydrates: 10g Fat: 22g Fiber: 3g Cholesterol: 90mg Sodium: 950mg Potassium: 500mg

Fish & Seafood

Grilled Lemon Garlic Salmon

Yield: 4 servings | **Prep time:** 10 mins | **Cook time:** 12 mins

Ingredients:

- 4 salmon fillets (6 oz each)
- 2 tbsp olive oil
- 4 cloves garlic, minced
- 2 tbsp fresh lemon juice
- Fresh parsley, for garnish
- 1 tsp lemon zest
- 1 tsp dried oregano
- 1/2 tsp salt
- 1/4 tsp black pepper

Directions:

1. Preheat grill to medium-high heat.
2. Combine olive oil, minced garlic, lemon juice, lemon zest, oregano, salt, and pepper in a bowl.
3. Place salmon fillets in a shallow dish and pour the marinade over them. Let marinate for 10 mins.
4. Grease grill grates and place salmon, skin-side down. Grill for 5-6 mins.
5. Carefully flip salmon and grill for another 5-6 mins, until desired doneness.
6. Remove from grill and garnish with parsley.
7. Serve hot with side dishes or salad.

Nutritional Information (per serving): Calories: 354 Protein: 38g Carbs: 1g Fat: 22g Fiber: 0g Cholesterol: 94mg Sodium: 345mg Potassium: 857mg

Baked Mediterranean Herb Crusted Cod

Yield: 4 servings | **Prep time:** 15 mins | **Cook time:** 20 mins

Ingredients:

- 4 cod fillets (6 oz each)
- 2 tbsp olive oil
- 2 tbsp lemon juice
- 2 cloves garlic, minced
- 1 tsp dried oregano
- 1 tsp dried basil
- Fresh parsley, for garnish
- 1/2 tsp salt
- 1/4 tsp black pepper
- 1/4 cup almond flour
- 1/4 cup grated Parmesan cheese
- Lemon wedges, for serving

Directions:

1. Preheat oven to 400°F (200°C) and line a baking sheet with parchment paper.
2. Place cod fillets on the prepared baking sheet.
3. In a small bowl, combine olive oil, lemon juice, minced garlic, oregano, basil, salt, and black pepper to make a marinade. Brush marinade over cod fillets, ensuring even coating.
4. In a separate bowl, mix almond flour and Parmesan cheese.
5. Sprinkle almond flour mixture over each cod fillet, pressing lightly to adhere.
6. Bake for 15-20 mins, until cod is cooked and flakes easily. Remove from oven and let it rest.
7. Serve with lemon wedges and garnish with fresh parsley.

Nutritional Information (per serving): Calories: 238 Protein: 34g Carbs: 2g Fat: 10g Fiber: 1g Cholesterol: 79mg Sodium: 491mg Potassium: 724mg

Lemon Butter Shrimp Skewers

Yield: 4 servings | **Prep time:** 15 mins | **Cook time:** 10 mins

Ingredients:

- 1.5 lbs large shrimp, peeled and deveined
- 4 tbsp melted unsalted butter
- 2 tbsp fresh lemon juice
- 2 cloves garlic, minced
- 1 tbsp chopped fresh parsley
- Fresh parsley, for garnish
- 1/2 tsp dried oregano
- 1/4 tsp salt
- 1/4 tsp black pepper
- Lemon wedges, for serving

Directions:

1. Preheat grill or oven broiler.
2. In a bowl, combine melted butter, lemon juice, minced garlic, chopped parsley, dried oregano, salt, and black pepper.
3. Thread shrimp onto skewers.
4. Brush shrimp skewers with lemon butter marinade, reserving some for basting.
5. Grill or broil for 2-3 mins per side, basting with reserved marinade.
6. Cook until shrimp turn pink and opaque.
7. Remove from heat and let them rest.
8. Serve with lemon wedges and garnish with fresh parsley.

Nutritional Information (per serving): Calories: 230 Protein: 30g Carbs: 1g Fat: 11g Fiber: 0g Cholesterol: 288mg Sodium: 364mg Potassium: 217mg

Grilled Garlic Butter Lobster Tails

Yield: 4 servings | **Prep time:** 10 minutes | **Cook time:** 8 minutes

Ingredients:

- 4 lobster tails
- 4 tbsp melted butter
- 4 cloves minced garlic
- Salt and pepper, to taste
- 1 tbsp chopped fresh parsley
- 1 tbsp lemon juice

Directions:

1. Preheat grill to medium-high heat.
2. Cut through the top shell of each lobster tail and spread the shells apart.
3. In a bowl, mix melted butter, minced garlic, parsley, lemon juice, salt, and pepper.
4. Brush the mixture over the lobster meat.
5. Grill lobster tails meat side down for 4 minutes.
6. Flip and grill for 3-4 more minutes until meat is opaque and cooked through.
7. Serve hot with lemon wedges.

Nutritional Information (per serving): Calories: 189 Protein: 26g Carbohydrates: 1g Fat: 9g Fiber: 0g Cholesterol: 128mg Sodium: 278mg Potassium: 285mg

Greek Style Baked Tilapia

Yield: 4 servings | **Prep time:** 10 mins | **Cook time:** 20 mins

Ingredients:

- 4 tilapia fillets (6 oz each)
- 2 tbsp olive oil
- 2 tbsp lemon juice
- 2 cloves garlic, minced
- 1 tsp dried oregano
- Lemon wedges, for serving
- 1/2 tsp salt
- 1/4 tsp black pepper
- 1/4 cup crumbled feta cheese
- 2 tbsp chopped Kalamata olives
- 2 tbsp chopped fresh parsley

Directions:

1. Preheat oven to 400°F (200°C).
2. Place tilapia fillets on a greased baking dish.
3. Mix olive oil, lemon juice, minced garlic, dried oregano, salt, and black pepper in a small bowl.
4. Drizzle the mixture over the tilapia fillets.
5. Sprinkle crumbled feta cheese, chopped Kalamata olives, and fresh parsley on top.
6. Bake for 15-20 mins until fish is cooked and flakes easily.
7. Remove from oven and let it rest.
8. Serve with lemon wedges.

Nutritional Information (per serving): Calories: 238 Protein: 36g Carbs: 2g Fat: 10g Fiber: 0g Cholesterol: 83mg Sodium: 529mg Potassium: 498mg

Spicy Garlic Grilled Shrimp

Yield: 4 servings | **Prep time:** 10 minutes | **Cook time:** 5 minutes

Ingredients:

- 1.5 pounds large shrimp, peeled and deveined
- 3 tablespoons olive oil
- 3 cloves garlic, minced
- 1 tablespoon lemon juice
- 1 teaspoon paprika
- Lemon wedges, for serving
- 1/2 teaspoon cayenne pepper (adjust to taste)
- 1/2 teaspoon salt
- 1/4 teaspoon black pepper
- Fresh parsley, for garnish

Directions:

1. Preheat the grill to medium-high heat.
2. In a bowl, combine olive oil, minced garlic, lemon juice, paprika, cayenne pepper, salt, and black pepper to make a marinade.
3. Add the shrimp to the marinade and toss until they are well coated. Let it marinate for 10 minutes.
4. Thread the shrimp onto skewers, piercing through the tail and head end to keep them secure.
5. Place the shrimp skewers on the preheated grill and cook for about 2-3 minutes per side until they turn pink and opaque.
6. Remove the shrimp skewers from the grill and let them rest for a minute.
7. Garnish with fresh parsley and serve with lemon wedges on the side.

Nutritional Information (per serving): Calories: 196 Protein: 24g Carbohydrates: 2g Fat: 10g Fiber: 0g Cholesterol: 239mg Sodium: 616mg Potassium: 199mgz

Mediterranean Tuna Salad Lettuce Wraps

Yield: 4 servings | **Prep time:** 15 minutes | **Cook time:** 0 minutes

Ingredients:

- 2 cans (5 ounces each) tuna, drained
- 1/4 cup diced cucumber
- 1/4 cup diced tomatoes
- 1/4 cup chopped Kalamata olives
- 2 tablespoons chopped red onion
- 8 large lettuce leaves (such as romaine or butter lettuce)
- 2 tablespoons chopped fresh parsley
- 2 tablespoons extra-virgin olive oil
- 1 tablespoon lemon juice
- 1 teaspoon Dijon mustard
- Salt and pepper, to taste

Directions:

1. In a bowl, flake the drained tuna with a fork.
2. Add diced cucumber, tomatoes, Kalamata olives, red onion, and fresh parsley to the tuna.
3. In a separate small bowl, whisk together extra-virgin olive oil, lemon juice, Dijon mustard, salt, and pepper to make a dressing.
4. Pour the dressing over the tuna mixture and toss to combine.
5. Spoon the tuna salad onto each lettuce leaf.
6. Wrap the lettuce leaves around the tuna salad to create lettuce wraps.
7. Serve the Mediterranean Tuna Salad Lettuce Wraps as a light and refreshing meal.

Nutritional Information (per serving): Calories: 210 Protein: 20g Carbohydrates: 4g Fat: 13g Fiber: 1g Cholesterol: 30mg Sodium: 460mg Potassium: 360mg

Greek Style Stuffed Squid

Yield: 4 servings | **Prep time:** 20 mins | **Cook time:** 30 mins

Ingredients:

- 8 small squid tubes
- 1/2 cup almond flour
- 1/4 cup grated Parmesan cheese
- 2 tbsp chopped fresh parsley
- 2 tbsp chopped Kalamata olives
- 2 tbsp chopped sun-dried tomatoes
- Lemon wedges, for serving
- 2 cloves garlic, minced
- 2 tbsp extra-virgin olive oil
- 1 tbsp lemon juice
- 1/2 tsp dried oregano
- Salt and pepper, to taste

Directions:

1. Preheat oven to 375°F (190°C). Clean squid tubes, rinse, and pat dry.
2. In a bowl, mix almond flour, grated Parmesan cheese, parsley, olives, sun-dried tomatoes, garlic, olive oil, lemon juice, oregano, salt, and pepper.
3. Stuff each squid tube with the mixture and secure with toothpicks.
4. Place stuffed squid in a greased baking dish.
5. Bake for 25-30 mins until squid is cooked and filling is golden brown.
6. Remove toothpicks before serving.
7. Serve with lemon wedges.

Nutritional Information (per serving): Calories: 225 Protein: 22g Carbs: 5g Fat: 13g Fiber: 1g Cholesterol: 229mg Sodium: 535mg Potassium: 367mg

Baked Lemon Herb Halibut

Yield: 4 servings | **Prep time:** 10 mins | **Cook time:** 15 mins

Ingredients:

- 4 halibut fillets (6 oz each)
- 2 tbsp olive oil
- 2 tbsp lemon juice
- 2 cloves garlic, minced
- Fresh parsley, for garnish
- 1 tsp dried thyme
- 1 tsp dried oregano
- Salt and pepper, to taste
- Lemon wedges, for serving

Directions:

1. Preheat oven to 400°F (200°C) and grease a baking dish.
2. Place halibut fillets in the dish.
3. In a small bowl, whisk together olive oil, lemon juice, garlic, thyme, oregano, salt, and pepper.
4. Pour the mixture over the halibut fillets.
5. Bake for 12-15 mins until halibut is cooked and flakes easily.
6. Let it rest for a minute.
7. Serve with lemon wedges and garnish with parsley.

Nutritional Information (per serving): Calories: 259 Protein: 34g Carbs: 1g Fat: 13g Fiber: 0g Cholesterol: 83mg Sodium: 179mg Potassium: 611mg

Moroccan Spiced Grilled Swordfish

Yield: 4 servings | **Prep time:** 15 mins | **Cook time:** 10 mins

Ingredients:

- 4 swordfish steaks (6 oz each)
- 2 tbsp olive oil
- 2 tsp ground cumin
- 2 tsp ground coriander
- 1 tsp ground paprika
- Fresh cilantro, for garnish
- 1/2 tsp ground cinnamon
- 1/2 tsp ground ginger
- 1/2 tsp salt
- 1/4 tsp black pepper
- Lemon wedges, for serving

Directions:

1. Preheat grill to medium-high heat.
2. Pat dry swordfish steaks and place on a plate.
3. In a small bowl, mix olive oil, cumin, coriander, paprika, cinnamon, ginger, salt, and black pepper.
4. Rub spice mixture evenly over swordfish steaks.
5. Grill for 4-5 mins per side until cooked through with grill marks.
6. Remove from grill and let it rest for a minute.
7. Serve with lemon wedges and garnish with cilantro.

Nutritional Information (per serving): Calories: 285 Protein: 33g Carbs: 2g Fat: 16g Fiber: 1g Cholesterol: 86mg Sodium: 362mg Potassium: 690mg

Shrimp and Avocado Salad with Feta

Yield: 4 servings | **Prep time:** 15 mins | **Cook time:** 5 mins

Ingredients:

- 1 lb shrimp, peeled and deveined
- 2 tbsp olive oil
- 1 tsp paprika
- 1/2 tsp garlic powder
- Salt and pepper, to taste
- 2 tbsp extra-virgin olive oil
- 4 cups mixed salad greens
- 1 avocado, diced
- 1/2 cup cherry tomatoes, halved
- 1/4 cup crumbled feta cheese
- 2 tbsp fresh lemon juice

Directions:

1. Toss shrimp with olive oil, paprika, garlic powder, salt, and pepper.
2. Cook shrimp in a skillet over medium-high heat for 2-3 mins per side until pink and cooked.
3. In a salad bowl, combine greens, avocado, tomatoes, and feta cheese.
4. Whisk lemon juice and extra-virgin olive oil to make the dressing.
5. Drizzle dressing over the salad and toss gently.
6. Divide salad among plates and top with cooked shrimp.
7. Serve immediately.

Nutritional Information (per serving): Calories: 284 Protein: 23g Carbs: 9g Fat: 18g Fiber: 5g Cholesterol: 191mg Sodium: 359mg Potassium: 683mg

Greek Style Grilled Octopus

Yield: 4 servings | **Prep time:** 10 minutes | **Cook time:** 30 minutes

Ingredients:

- 2 pounds octopus tentacles
- 1/4 cup olive oil
- 2 cloves garlic, minced
- 2 tablespoons lemon juice
- Fresh parsley, for garnish
- 1 teaspoon dried oregano
- Salt and pepper, to taste
- Lemon wedges, for serving

Directions:

1. Preheat grill to medium-high heat.
2. Rinse the octopus tentacles under cold water and pat dry with paper towels.
3. In a bowl, whisk together olive oil, minced garlic, lemon juice, dried oregano, salt, and pepper.
4. Place the octopus tentacles in a shallow dish and pour the marinade over them, making sure they are well coated. Let marinate for 10 minutes.
5. Grill the octopus tentacles for about 15 minutes, turning occasionally, until they are tender and charred.
6. Remove from the grill and let it rest for a few minutes.
7. Slice the grilled octopus tentacles into bite-sized pieces.
8. Serve with lemon wedges and garnish with fresh parsley.

Nutritional Information (per serving): Calories: 175 Protein: 25g Carbohydrates: 1g Fat: 8g Fiber: 0g Cholesterol: 134mg Sodium: 292mg Potassium: 554mg

Pan-Seared Scallops with Lemon Caper Sauce

Yield: 4 servings | **Prep time:** 10 minutes | **Cook time:** 10 minutes

Ingredients:

- 1 lb scallops
- 2 tbsp olive oil
- Salt and pepper
- 2 tbsp butter
- 2 tbsp chopped fresh parsley
- 2 cloves garlic, minced
- 2 tbsp capers, drained
- 2 tbsp fresh lemon juice

Directions:

1. Season scallops with salt and pepper.
2. Heat olive oil in a skillet over medium-high heat.
3. Cook scallops for 2-3 minutes per side until golden brown. Remove and set aside.
4. In the same skillet, melt butter and add minced garlic. Cook for 1 minute.
5. Stir in capers and lemon juice, cook for 1-2 minutes until sauce thickens slightly.
6. Return scallops to the skillet, toss in the sauce to coat.
7. Sprinkle with chopped parsley.
8. Serve immediately.

Nutritional Information (per serving): Calories: 209 Protein: 20g Carbohydrates: 2g Fat: 13g Fiber: 0g Cholesterol: 57mg Sodium: 540mg Potassium: 346mg

Italian Style Grilled Sardines

Yield: 4 servings | **Prep time:** 10 minutes | **Cook time:** 8 minutes

Ingredients:

- 8 fresh sardines
- 2 tbsp olive oil
- 2 cloves garlic, minced
- Salt and pepper, to taste
- 1 tbsp chopped parsley
- 1 tbsp lemon juice

Directions:

1. Preheat grill to medium-high heat.
2. Brush sardines with olive oil, garlic, parsley, lemon juice, salt, and pepper.
3. Grill sardines for 4 minutes per side until cooked through and grill marks appear.
4. Remove from grill and serve hot.

Nutritional Information (per serving): Calories: 187 Protein: 19g Carbohydrates: 0g Fat: 12g Fiber: 0g Cholesterol: 77mg Sodium: 59mg Potassium: 346mg

Lemon Dill Baked Cod

Yield: 4 servings | **Prep time:** 10 minutes | **Cook time:** 15 minutes

Ingredients:

- 4 cod fillets
- 2 tablespoons olive oil
- 2 tablespoons fresh lemon juice
- Salt and pepper, to taste
- 2 teaspoons lemon zest
- 2 cloves garlic, minced
- 1 tablespoon chopped fresh dill

Directions:

1. Preheat the oven to 400°F (200°C) and lightly grease a baking dish.
2. Place the cod fillets in the baking dish.
3. In a small bowl, whisk together the olive oil, lemon juice, lemon zest, minced garlic, chopped dill, salt, and pepper.
4. Pour the lemon dill mixture over the cod fillets, making sure they are evenly coated.
5. Bake in the preheated oven for about 15 minutes or until the cod is cooked through and flakes easily with a fork.
6. Remove from the oven and serve hot.

Nutritional Information (per serving): Calories: 191 Protein: 29g Carbohydrates: 1g Fat: 8g Fiber: 0g Cholesterol: 62mg Sodium: 102mg Potassium: 680mg

Greek Shrimp and Zucchini Skillet

Yield: 4 servings | **Prep time:** 10 minutes | **Cook time:** 15 minutes

Ingredients:

- 1 lb shrimp, peeled and deveined
- 2 medium zucchini, sliced
- 1 bell pepper, sliced
- 1 small onion, thinly sliced
- 3 cloves garlic, minced
- Fresh parsley, for garnish
- 2 tbsp olive oil
- 1 tbsp lemon juice
- 1 tsp dried oregano
- 1/2 tsp dried thyme
- Salt and pepper, to taste

Directions:

1. Heat olive oil in a skillet. Sauté zucchini, bell pepper, and onion until tender-crisp.
2. Add garlic, oregano, thyme, salt, and pepper. Cook for 1 minute.
3. Push vegetables to the side and add shrimp. Cook until pink and cooked through.
4. Drizzle with lemon juice and toss everything together.
5. Remove from heat and garnish with parsley.
6. Serve hot as is or over cauliflower rice or zucchini noodles, if desired.

Nutritional Information (per serving): Calories: 197 Protein: 26g Carbohydrates: 7g Fat: 7g Fiber: 2g Cholesterol: 191mg Sodium: 337mg Potassium: 528mg

Mediterranean Style Mussels in Tomato Broth
Yield: 4 servings | **Prep time:** 10 minutes | **Cook time:** 15 minutes

Ingredients:

- 2 lbs fresh mussels
- 1 tbsp olive oil
- 1 small onion, finely chopped
- 2 cloves garlic, minced
- 1 cup diced tomatoes
- Salt and pepper, to taste
- 1/4 cup dry white wine
- 1/4 cup chicken or vegetable broth
- 2 tbsp chopped fresh parsley
- 1 tbsp lemon juice

Directions:

1. Clean and debeard the mussels, discarding any that are open or damaged.
2. In a large pot, heat olive oil over medium heat. Add chopped onion and minced garlic, and sauté until softened.
3. Add diced tomatoes, white wine, and broth to the pot. Bring to a simmer.
4. Add the cleaned mussels to the pot and cover. Cook for about 5-7 minutes, or until the mussels open.
5. Discard any unopened mussels. Stir in chopped parsley and lemon juice. Season with salt and pepper to taste.
6. Serve the mussels in bowls with the tomato broth. Enjoy!

Nutritional Information (per serving): Calories: 231 Protein: 25g Carbohydrates: 10g Fat: 8g Fiber: 2g Cholesterol: 48mg Sodium: 596mg Potassium: 654mg

Tuscan Herb Baked Salmon
Yield: 4 servings | **Prep time:** 10 minutes | **Cook time:** 15 minutes

Ingredients:

- 4 salmon fillets
- 2 tbsp olive oil
- 2 cloves garlic, minced
- 1 tsp dried basil
- 1 tsp dried oregano
- Fresh parsley, for garnish
- 1/2 tsp dried thyme
- 1/2 tsp dried rosemary
- Salt and pepper, to taste
- Lemon wedges, for serving

Directions:

1. Preheat the oven to 400°F (200°C). Line a baking sheet with parchment paper.
2. Place the salmon fillets on the prepared baking sheet.
3. In a small bowl, combine olive oil, minced garlic, dried basil, dried oregano, dried thyme, dried rosemary, salt, and pepper. Mix well.
4. Brush the herb mixture over the salmon fillets, coating them evenly.
5. Bake the salmon in the preheated oven for about 12-15 minutes, or until cooked through and flakes easily with a fork.
6. Remove the salmon from the oven and let it rest for a few minutes.
7. Serve the Tuscan herb baked salmon with lemon wedges. Garnish with fresh parsley.

Nutritional Information (per serving): Calories: 322 Protein: 35g Carbohydrates: 1g Fat: 19g Fiber: 0g Cholesterol: 94mg Sodium: 137mg Potassium: 843mg

Spicy Garlic Lime Grilled Shrimp Skewers

Yield: 4 servings | **Prep time:** 20 minutes | **Cook time:** 8 minutes

Ingredients:

- 1 lb large shrimp, peeled and deveined
- 3 cloves garlic, minced
- 2 tbsp olive oil
- 2 tbsp lime juice
- Wooden or metal skewers
- 1 tsp paprika
- 1/2 tsp chili powder
- 1/2 tsp cayenne pepper (adjust to taste)
- Salt and pepper, to taste

Directions:

1. In a bowl, combine minced garlic, olive oil, lime juice, paprika, chili powder, cayenne pepper, salt, and pepper. Mix well to make the marinade.
2. Add the shrimp to the marinade and toss to coat. Allow the shrimp to marinate for at least 10 minutes.
3. Preheat the grill to medium-high heat.
4. Thread the marinated shrimp onto skewers, dividing them evenly.
5. Place the shrimp skewers on the preheated grill. Cook for about 3-4 minutes per side, or until the shrimp are opaque and cooked through.
6. Remove the shrimp skewers from the grill and serve hot.

Nutritional Information (per serving): Calories: 153 Protein: 23g Carbohydrates: 2g Fat: 6g Fiber: 0g Cholesterol: 214mg Sodium: 194mg Potassium: 152mg

Mediterranean Tuna Stuffed Bell Peppers

Yield: 4 servings | **Prep time:** 15 minutes | **Cook time:** 25 minutes

Ingredients:

- 4 bell peppers (any color), tops removed and seeds removed
- 2 cans (5 oz each) tuna in water, drained
- 1/4 cup diced red onion
- 1/4 cup diced cucumber
- 1/4 cup diced cherry tomatoes
- Optional: crumbled feta cheese for topping
- 1/4 cup chopped Kalamata olives
- 2 tbsp chopped fresh parsley
- 2 tbsp extra-virgin olive oil
- 1 tbsp lemon juice
- 1/2 tsp dried oregano
- Salt and pepper, to taste

Directions:

1. Preheat the oven to 375°F (190°C).
2. In a large mixing bowl, combine tuna, red onion, cucumber, cherry tomatoes, Kalamata olives, parsley, olive oil, lemon juice, dried oregano, salt, and pepper. Mix well to combine.
3. Fill each bell pepper with the tuna mixture, pressing it down lightly.
4. Place the stuffed bell peppers in a baking dish. If desired, sprinkle crumbled feta cheese on top.
5. Bake in the preheated oven for 20-25 minutes, or until the bell peppers are tender and the filling is heated through.
6. Remove from the oven and let cool for a few minutes before serving.

Nutritional Information (per serving): Calories: 199 Protein: 21g Carbohydrates: 10g Fat: 9g Fiber: 3g Cholesterol: 34mg Sodium: 570mg Potassium: 442mg

Side dishes

Greek Salad with Feta Cheese

Yield: 4 servings | **Prep time:** 15 minutes | **Cook time:** 0 minutes

Ingredients:

- 2 large cucumbers, diced
- 4 medium tomatoes, diced
- 1 small red onion, thinly sliced
- 1 green bell pepper, diced
- 1/2 cup Kalamata olives, pitted
- Salt and black pepper to taste
- 4 ounces feta cheese, crumbled
- 2 tablespoons extra virgin olive oil
- 1 tablespoon red wine vinegar
- 1 teaspoon dried oregano

Directions:

1. In a large salad bowl, combine the diced cucumbers, tomatoes, red onion, bell pepper, and Kalamata olives.
2. In a small bowl, whisk together the olive oil, red wine vinegar, dried oregano, salt, and black pepper.
3. Pour the dressing over the salad and toss gently to coat all the ingredients.
4. Sprinkle the crumbled feta cheese over the salad.
5. Serve immediately or refrigerate for later use.

Nutritional Information: (per serving) Calories: 190 Protein: 6g Carbohydrates: 12g Fat: 14g Fiber: 3g Cholesterol: 25mg Sodium: 520mg Potassium: 430mg

Roasted Asparagus with Lemon and Parmesan

Yield: 4 servings | **Prep time:** 5 minutes | **Cook time:** 15 minutes

Ingredients:

- 1 pound asparagus spears, tough ends trimmed
- 2 tablespoons extra virgin olive oil
- Salt and black pepper to taste
- 1 lemon, zested and juiced
- 2 cloves garlic, minced
- 1/4 cup grated Parmesan cheese

Directions:

1. Preheat the oven to 425°F (220°C).
2. Place the asparagus spears on a baking sheet lined with parchment paper.
3. Drizzle the asparagus with olive oil, lemon juice, and minced garlic. Toss to coat evenly.
4. Sprinkle the lemon zest, grated Parmesan cheese, salt, and black pepper over the asparagus.
5. Roast in the preheated oven for about 12-15 minutes or until the asparagus is tender and slightly browned.
6. Remove from the oven and transfer the roasted asparagus to a serving dish.
7. Serve hot as a side dish.

Nutritional Information: (per serving) Calories: 100 Protein: 4g Carbohydrates: 5g Fat: 8g Fiber: 2g Cholesterol: 4mg Sodium: 120mg Potassium: 260mg

Zucchini Noodles with Pesto

Yield: 4 servings | **Prep time:** 15 minutes | **Cook time:** 5 minutes

Ingredients:

- 4 medium zucchini
- 1 cup fresh basil leaves
- 1/4 cup pine nuts
- 2 cloves garlic
- 1/4 cup grated Parmesan cheese
- 1/4 cup extra virgin olive oil
- Salt and black pepper to taste
- Optional toppings: cherry tomatoes, sliced olives, additional Parmesan cheese

Directions:

1. Trim the ends of the zucchini and spiralize them into noodle-like strands using a spiralizer or julienne peeler. Set aside.
2. In a food processor, combine the basil leaves, pine nuts, garlic, grated Parmesan cheese, olive oil, salt, and black pepper. Process until smooth and well combined.
3. Heat a large skillet over medium heat. Add the zucchini noodles and cook for about 2-3 minutes, tossing gently with tongs, until slightly softened.
4. Remove the skillet from heat and add the pesto sauce to the zucchini noodles. Toss until the noodles are coated evenly.
5. Divide the zucchini noodles into serving plates. If desired, top with cherry tomatoes, sliced olives, and additional Parmesan cheese.
6. Serve immediately as a light and flavorful side dish.

Nutritional Information: (per serving) Calories: 180 Protein: 6g Carbohydrates: 8g Fat: 15g Fiber: 3g Cholesterol: 4mg Sodium: 150mg Potassium: 580mg

Cauliflower Tabbouleh

Yield: 4 servings | **Prep time:** 15 minutes | **Cook time:** 0 minutes

Ingredients:

- 1 small head cauliflower
- 1 cup cherry tomatoes, halved
- 1/2 cup cucumber, diced
- 1/4 cup red onion, finely chopped
- Salt and black pepper to taste
- 1/4 cup fresh parsley, finely chopped
- 2 tablespoons fresh mint, finely chopped
- 2 tablespoons lemon juice
- 2 tablespoons extra virgin olive oil

Directions:

1. Remove the leaves from the cauliflower head and cut it into florets. Place the florets in a food processor and pulse until they resemble rice-like grains. Transfer the cauliflower "rice" to a large mixing bowl.
2. To the bowl, add the cherry tomatoes, cucumber, red onion, parsley, and mint. Toss gently to combine.
3. In a small bowl, whisk together the lemon juice, olive oil, salt, and black pepper.
4. Pour the dressing over the cauliflower mixture and toss until everything is evenly coated.
5. Allow the tabbouleh to sit for a few minutes to let the flavors meld together.
6. Serve the cauliflower tabbouleh chilled or at room temperature.

Nutritional Information: (per serving) Calories: 90 Protein: 4g Carbohydrates: 8g Fat: 6g Fiber: 3g Cholesterol: 0mg Sodium: 50mg Potassium: 570mg

Grilled Eggplant with Tahini Sauce

Yield: 4 servings | **Prep time:** 10 minutes | **Cook time:** 10 minutes

Ingredients:

- 2 medium eggplants
- 2 tablespoons olive oil
- 1/2 teaspoon salt
- 1/4 teaspoon black pepper
- 1 tablespoon chopped fresh parsley (for garnish)
- 1/4 cup tahini
- 2 tablespoons lemon juice
- 1 clove garlic, minced
- 2 tablespoons water

Directions:

1. Preheat the grill to medium-high heat.
2. Slice the eggplants into rounds or lengthwise, about 1/2-inch thick.
3. Brush both sides of the eggplant slices with olive oil and season with salt and black pepper.
4. Grill the eggplant slices for about 3-4 minutes per side until grill marks appear and the eggplant is tender.
5. While the eggplant is grilling, prepare the tahini sauce. In a small bowl, whisk together the tahini, lemon juice, minced garlic, and water until smooth and creamy.
6. Once the eggplant is cooked, remove from the grill and arrange on a serving platter.
7. Drizzle the tahini sauce over the grilled eggplant slices and garnish with chopped fresh parsley.
8. Serve the grilled eggplant warm as a delicious keto Mediterranean side dish.

Nutritional Information: (per serving) Calories: 140 Protein: 3g Carbohydrates: 9g Fat: 11g Fiber: 4g Cholesterol: 0mg Sodium: 330mg Potassium: 420mg

Tomato and Mozzarella Caprese Salad

Yield: 4 servings | **Prep time:** 10 minutes | **Cook time:** 0 minutes

Ingredients:

- 4 medium tomatoes, sliced
- 8 ounces fresh mozzarella cheese, sliced
- 1/4 cup fresh basil leaves
- Salt and black pepper to taste
- 2 tablespoons extra virgin olive oil
- 1 tablespoon balsamic vinegar

Directions:

1. Arrange the tomato slices and mozzarella slices on a serving platter, alternating between them.
2. Tuck the fresh basil leaves in between the tomato and mozzarella slices.
3. Drizzle the extra virgin olive oil and balsamic vinegar over the salad.
4. Sprinkle salt and black pepper to taste.
5. Allow the flavors to meld together for a few minutes before serving.
6. Serve the tomato and mozzarella Caprese salad as a refreshing and light side dish.

Nutritional Information: (per serving) Calories: 220 Protein: 11g Carbohydrates: 6g Fat: 17g Fiber: 1g Cholesterol: 30mg Sodium: 280mg Potassium: 350mg

Stuffed Bell Peppers with Ground Turkey and Feta

Yield: 4 servings | **Prep time:** 15 minutes | **Cook time:** 35 minutes

Ingredients:

- 4 bell peppers
- 1 tbsp olive oil
- 1 lb ground turkey
- 1 small onion, diced
- 2 cloves garlic, minced
- 1/4 cup chopped fresh parsley
- 1 tsp dried oregano
- 1/2 tsp each dried basil and thyme
- 1/2 tsp salt
- 1/4 tsp black pepper
- 1/2 cup crumbled feta cheese

Directions:

1. Preheat the oven to 375°F (190°C).
2. Hollow out the bell peppers and set them upright in a baking dish.
3. Heat olive oil in a skillet, then cook ground turkey, onion, and garlic until turkey is browned.
4. Add dried herbs, salt, and pepper, and cook for 2-3 minutes.
5. Remove from heat, let it cool slightly, then stir in feta cheese.
6. Fill the bell peppers with the turkey mixture.
7. Bake for 25-30 minutes until peppers are tender and filling is cooked.
8. Garnish with chopped parsley.
9. Serve and enjoy!

Nutritional Information: (per serving) Calories: 280 Protein: 24g Carbohydrates: 14g Fat: 15g Fiber: 4g Cholesterol: 80mg Sodium: 510mg Potassium: 780mg

Cucumber and Avocado Salad

Yield: 4 servings | **Prep time:** 10 minutes | **Cook time:** 0 minutes

Ingredients:

- 2 large cucumbers
- 2 avocados
- 1/4 cup red onion, thinly sliced
- Salt and black pepper to taste
- 2 tablespoons fresh lemon juice
- 2 tablespoons extra virgin olive oil
- 1 tablespoon chopped fresh dill

Directions:

1. Peel and slice the cucumbers into thin rounds. Place them in a large mixing bowl.
2. Cut the avocados in half, remove the pits, and scoop out the flesh. Slice the avocado into cubes or slices and add them to the bowl with the cucumbers.
3. Add the sliced red onion to the bowl.
4. In a small bowl, whisk together the lemon juice, olive oil, chopped fresh dill, salt, and black pepper.
5. Pour the dressing over the cucumber and avocado mixture. Gently toss to coat all the ingredients.
6. Adjust the seasoning if needed.
7. Allow the salad to sit for a few minutes to let the flavors meld together.
8. Serve the cucumber and avocado salad as a refreshing and nutritious keto Mediterranean side dish.

Nutritional Information: (per serving) Calories: 190 Protein: 3g Carbohydrates: 11g Fat: 17g Fiber: 7g Cholesterol: 0mg Sodium: 10mg Potassium: 780mg

Roasted Brussels Sprouts with Balsamic Glaze

Yield: 4 servings | **Prep time:** 10 minutes | **Cook time:** 25 minutes

Ingredients:

- 1 pound Brussels sprouts
- 2 tablespoons olive oil
- 1 tablespoon low-carb sweetener (optional)
- Salt and black pepper to taste
- 2 tablespoons balsamic vinegar

Directions:

1. Preheat the oven to 425°F (220°C). Line a baking sheet with parchment paper.
2. Trim the stems of the Brussels sprouts and cut them in half lengthwise.
3. In a large bowl, toss the Brussels sprouts with olive oil, salt, and black pepper until well coated.
4. Spread the Brussels sprouts in a single layer on the prepared baking sheet.
5. Roast in the preheated oven for 20-25 minutes, or until the Brussels sprouts are tender and lightly browned, stirring once halfway through.
6. In a small saucepan, combine balsamic vinegar and low-carb sweetener (if using). Bring to a simmer over medium heat and cook for 3-4 minutes, or until the glaze thickens slightly.
7. Remove the roasted Brussels sprouts from the oven and drizzle the balsamic glaze over them. Toss to coat evenly.
8. Serve the roasted Brussels sprouts with balsamic glaze as a flavorful and healthy keto Mediterranean side dish.

Nutritional Information: (per serving) Calories: 110 Protein: 4g Carbohydrates: 11g Fat: 7g Fiber: 4g Cholesterol: 0mg Sodium: 25mg Potassium: 450mg

Spinach and Feta Stuffed Mushrooms

Yield: 4 servings | **Prep time:** 15 minutes | **Cook time:** 20 minutes

Ingredients:

- 16 large mushrooms, stems removed
- 1 tablespoon olive oil
- 2 cups fresh spinach, chopped
- 2 cloves garlic, minced
- Salt and black pepper to taste
- 1/4 cup crumbled feta cheese
- 2 tablespoons grated Parmesan cheese
- 1 tablespoon chopped fresh parsley

Directions:

1. Preheat the oven to 375°F (190°C) and line a baking sheet with parchment paper.
2. Place the mushrooms cap-side down on the baking sheet.
3. Sauté the chopped spinach and minced garlic in olive oil until wilted, then let it cool slightly.
4. In a bowl, combine the cooked spinach mixture, crumbled feta cheese, grated Parmesan cheese, chopped fresh parsley, salt, and black pepper.
5. Spoon the spinach and feta mixture into the mushroom caps.
6. Bake for 18-20 minutes until the mushrooms are tender and the filling is golden and bubbly.
7. Let the stuffed mushrooms cool for a few minutes.
8. Serve and enjoy as a keto Mediterranean appetizer or side dish.

Nutritional Information: (per serving) Calories: 90 Protein: 5g Carbohydrates: 6g Fat: 6g Fiber: 2g Cholesterol: 10mg Sodium: 170mg Potassium: 520mg

Roasted Red Pepper and Feta Dip

Yield: 4 servings | **Prep time:** 10 minutes | **Cook time:** 20 minutes

Ingredients:

- 2 large red bell peppers
- 1 tablespoon olive oil
- 1/2 cup crumbled feta cheese
- 1/4 cup Greek yogurt
- Salt and black pepper to taste
- 2 tablespoons chopped fresh parsley
- 1 clove garlic, minced
- 1/2 teaspoon ground cumin

Directions:

1. Preheat the broiler. Cut the red bell peppers in half and remove the seeds and stems.
2. Place the peppers on a baking sheet, cut-side down, and broil for about 10 minutes until charred.
3. Transfer the peppers to a bowl, cover with plastic wrap, and let them steam for 10 minutes.
4. Peel off the charred skin from the peppers.
5. In a food processor or blender, combine the roasted red peppers, olive oil, feta cheese, Greek yogurt, parsley, garlic, cumin, salt, and black pepper. Blend until smooth.
6. Transfer the dip to a serving bowl and garnish with additional parsley, if desired.
7. Serve with keto-friendly vegetable sticks or low-carb crackers. Enjoy!

Nutritional Information: (per serving) Calories: 90 Protein: 4g Carbohydrates: 6g Fat: 6g Fiber: 2g Cholesterol: 15mg Sodium: 200mg Potassium: 250mg

Grilled Portobello Mushrooms with Herbed Goat Cheese

Yield: 4 servings | **Prep time:** 10 minutes | **Cook time:** 12 minutes

Ingredients:

- 4 large portobello mushrooms
- 2 tablespoons olive oil
- 4 ounces herbed goat cheese
- Salt and black pepper to taste
- 2 tablespoons chopped fresh basil
- 2 tablespoons chopped fresh parsley
- 1 clove garlic, minced

Directions:

1. Preheat the grill to medium-high heat.
2. Clean the portobello mushrooms and remove the stems. Brush both sides of the mushrooms with olive oil.
3. In a small bowl, combine the herbed goat cheese, chopped fresh basil, chopped fresh parsley, minced garlic, salt, and black pepper. Mix well.
4. Place the mushrooms on the grill, gill-side down, and cook for 4-5 minutes until grill marks appear.
5. Flip the mushrooms and spoon the herbed goat cheese mixture into the mushroom caps.
6. Continue grilling for another 4-5 minutes, or until the mushrooms are tender and the cheese is slightly melted.
7. Remove the mushrooms from the grill and let them cool for a minute before serving.
8. Serve the grilled portobello mushrooms with herbed goat cheese as a flavorful keto Mediterranean side dish or appetizer.

Nutritional Information: (per serving) Calories: 180 Protein: 8g Carbohydrates: 7g Fat: 14g Fiber: 2g Cholesterol: 15mg Sodium: 230mg Potassium: 700mg

Greek-style Green Beans

Yield: 4 servings | **Prep time:** 10 minutes | **Cook time:** 25 minutes

Ingredients:

- 1 pound green beans, trimmed
- 2 tablespoons olive oil
- 1 small onion, finely chopped
- 2 cloves garlic, minced
- 1 can (14 ounces) diced tomatoes
- Fresh lemon wedges, for serving
- 1 teaspoon dried oregano
- 1/2 teaspoon dried basil
- Salt and black pepper to taste
- 2 tablespoons crumbled feta cheese (optional, for serving)

Directions:

1. Boil green beans until tender-crisp, then drain.
2. Sauté onion and garlic in olive oil until translucent.
3. Add diced tomatoes, oregano, basil, salt, and pepper to the skillet. Simmer for 10 minutes.
4. Toss cooked green beans with tomato mixture and cook for an additional 5 minutes.
5. Transfer to a serving dish.
6. Optional: Sprinkle with crumbled feta cheese.
7. Serve warm with fresh lemon wedges.

Nutritional Information: (per serving) Calories: 120 Protein: 3g Carbohydrates: 12g Fat: 7g Fiber: 4g Cholesterol: 0mg Sodium: 270mg Potassium: 450mg

Roasted Cauliflower with Garlic and Lemon

Yield: 4 servings | **Prep time:** 10 minutes | **Cook time:** 25 minutes

Ingredients:

- 1 large head of cauliflower, cut into florets
- 3 tablespoons olive oil
- 4 cloves garlic, minced
- Zest of 1 lemon
- Fresh parsley, chopped (for garnish)
- Juice of 1 lemon
- 1 teaspoon dried thyme
- Salt and black pepper to taste

Directions:

1. Preheat the oven to 425°F (220°C) and line a baking sheet with parchment paper.
2. In a large bowl, combine the cauliflower florets, olive oil, minced garlic, lemon zest, lemon juice, dried thyme, salt, and black pepper. Toss until the cauliflower is evenly coated.
3. Spread the cauliflower in a single layer on the prepared baking sheet.
4. Roast in the preheated oven for 20-25 minutes, or until the cauliflower is tender and lightly browned, stirring once halfway through.
5. Remove from the oven and transfer the roasted cauliflower to a serving dish.
6. Garnish with fresh chopped parsley.
7. Serve hot as a delicious side dish.

Nutritional Information: (per serving) Calories: 120 Protein: 5g Carbohydrates: 10g Fat: 8g Fiber: 4g Cholesterol: 0mg Sodium: 80mg Potassium: 560mg

Mediterranean Roasted Vegetables

Yield: 4 servings | **Prep time:** 10 minutes | **Cook time:** 25 minutes

Ingredients:

- 1 medium eggplant, cut into cubes
- 1 medium zucchini, sliced
- 1 red bell pepper, seeded and sliced
- 1 yellow bell pepper, seeded and sliced
- 1 red onion, sliced
- 10 cherry tomatoes
- Fresh parsley, chopped (for garnish)
- 3 tablespoons olive oil
- 3 cloves garlic, minced
- 1 teaspoon dried oregano
- 1/2 teaspoon dried thyme
- Salt and black pepper to taste

Directions:

1. Preheat the oven to 425°F (220°C) and line a baking sheet with parchment paper.
2. In a large bowl, combine the eggplant, zucchini, bell peppers, red onion, cherry tomatoes, olive oil, minced garlic, dried oregano, dried thyme, salt, and black pepper. Toss until the vegetables are evenly coated.
3. Spread the vegetables in a single layer on the prepared baking sheet.
4. Roast in the preheated oven for 20-25 minutes, or until the vegetables are tender and lightly browned, stirring once halfway through.
5. Remove from the oven and transfer the roasted vegetables to a serving dish.
6. Garnish with fresh chopped parsley.
7. Serve hot as a flavorful side dish.

Nutritional Information: (per serving) Calories: 130 Protein: 3g Carbohydrates: 15g Fat: 8g Fiber: 6g Cholesterol: 0mg Sodium: 10mg Potassium: 560mg

Artichoke and Tomato Salad

Yield: 4 servings | **Prep time:** 10 minutes | **Cook time:** 0 minutes

Ingredients:

- 1 can (14 oz) artichoke hearts, drained and quartered
- 2 cups cherry tomatoes, halved
- 1/4 cup sliced red onion
- Salt and black pepper to taste
- 1/4 cup chopped fresh basil
- 2 tbsp extra-virgin olive oil
- 1 tbsp lemon juice
- 1 clove garlic, minced

Directions:

1. In a large bowl, combine artichoke hearts, cherry tomatoes, red onion, and fresh basil.
2. In a small bowl, whisk together olive oil, lemon juice, garlic, salt, and black pepper to make the dressing.
3. Pour the dressing over the salad ingredients and toss to coat evenly.
4. Serve chilled or at room temperature.

Nutritional Information: (per serving) Calories: 110 Protein: 3g Carbohydrates: 10g Fat: 7g Fiber: 4g Cholesterol: 0mg Sodium: 290mg Potassium: 430mg

Lemon Garlic Roasted Broccoli

Yield: 4 servings | **Prep time:** 5 minutes | **Cook time:** 20 minutes

Ingredients:

- 1 head of broccoli, cut into florets
- 2 tablespoons olive oil
- 2 cloves garlic, minced
- Salt and black pepper to taste
- 1 tablespoon lemon juice
- Zest of 1 lemon

Directions:

1. Preheat the oven to 425°F (220°C) and line a baking sheet with parchment paper.
2. In a large bowl, toss the broccoli florets with olive oil, minced garlic, lemon juice, lemon zest, salt, and black pepper.
3. Spread the seasoned broccoli in a single layer on the prepared baking sheet.
4. Roast in the preheated oven for about 20 minutes, or until the broccoli is tender and lightly browned, stirring halfway through cooking.
5. Remove from the oven and serve hot.

Nutritional Information: (per serving) Calories: 90 Protein: 4g Carbohydrates: 8g Fat: 6g Fiber: 3g Cholesterol: 0mg Sodium: 50mg Potassium: 470mg

Marinated Olives and Feta

Yield: 4 servings | **Prep time:** 10 minutes | **Cook time:** 0 minutes

Ingredients:

- 1 cup mixed olives (such as Kalamata, green, or black olives)
- 1/2 cup feta cheese, crumbled
- 2 tablespoons extra virgin olive oil
- Fresh parsley, for garnish (optional)
- 1 tablespoon lemon juice
- 1 clove garlic, minced
- 1 teaspoon dried oregano
- 1/4 teaspoon red pepper flakes (optional)

Directions:

1. In a bowl, combine the olives, crumbled feta cheese, extra virgin olive oil, lemon juice, minced garlic, dried oregano, and red pepper flakes (if using). Mix well to coat the olives and feta evenly with the marinade.
2. Allow the mixture to marinate for at least 30 minutes to allow the flavors to meld together.
3. Garnish with fresh parsley, if desired, and serve as an appetizer or as part of a mezze platter.

Nutritional Information: (per serving) Calories: 160 Protein: 4g Carbohydrates: 2g Fat: 16g Fiber: 1g Cholesterol: 15mg Sodium: 520mg Potassium: 40mg

Roasted Garlic and Herb Mushrooms

Yield: 4 servings | **Prep time:** 10 minutes | **Cook time:** 20 minutes

Ingredients:

- 1 lb mushrooms, such as cremini or button mushrooms
- 3 tablespoons olive oil
- 4 cloves garlic, minced
- Fresh parsley, for garnish (optional)
- 1 tablespoon fresh thyme leaves
- 1 teaspoon dried rosemary
- Salt and pepper, to taste

Directions:

1. Preheat the oven to 400°F (200°C). Line a baking sheet with parchment paper.
2. Clean the mushrooms and trim the stems if necessary. If using larger mushrooms, you can cut them into halves or quarters.
3. In a bowl, combine the olive oil, minced garlic, fresh thyme leaves, dried rosemary, salt, and pepper. Mix well.
4. Add the mushrooms to the bowl and toss to coat them evenly with the garlic and herb mixture.
5. Arrange the mushrooms in a single layer on the prepared baking sheet.
6. Roast the mushrooms in the preheated oven for about 20 minutes or until they are tender and golden brown, stirring once or twice during cooking.
7. Remove from the oven and garnish with fresh parsley, if desired. Serve hot.

Nutritional Information: (per serving) Calories: 110 Protein: 3g Carbohydrates: 4g Fat: 9g Fiber: 1g Cholesterol: 0mg Sodium: 5mg Potassium: 400mg

Eggplant and Tomato Stacks with Mozzarella

Yield: 4 servings | **Prep time:** 15 minutes | **Cook time:** 20 minutes

Ingredients:

- 1 large eggplant
- 2 large tomatoes
- 8 ounces fresh mozzarella cheese
- 2 tablespoons olive oil
- Fresh basil leaves, for garnish (optional)
- 2 cloves garlic, minced
- 1 teaspoon dried basil
- Salt and pepper, to taste

Directions:

1. Preheat oven to 400°F (200°C). Line a baking sheet with parchment paper.
2. Slice eggplant and tomatoes into 1/4-inch rounds.
3. Place eggplant on baking sheet, brush with olive oil, and sprinkle with garlic, dried basil, salt, and pepper.
4. Bake for 15-20 minutes until tender and golden brown.
5. Layer eggplant, tomato, and mozzarella to create stacks.
6. Return stacks to the oven for 5 minutes until cheese melts.
7. Garnish with fresh basil leaves, if desired. Serve warm.

Nutritional Information: (per serving) Calories: 210 Protein: 12g Carbohydrates: 11g Fat: 14g Fiber: 4g Cholesterol: 30mg Sodium: 270mg Potassium: 520mg

Vegetarian Meals

Roasted Eggplant with Feta and Olives

Yield: 4 servings | **Prep time:** 15 mins | **Cook time:** 30 mins

Ingredients:

- 2 medium eggplants
- 2 tbsp olive oil
- 1 tsp dried oregano
- 1/2 tsp garlic powder
- Fresh parsley, for garnish
- Salt and pepper, to taste
- 1/2 cup crumbled feta cheese
- 1/4 cup sliced Kalamata olives

Directions:

1. Preheat oven to 400°F (200°C). Line a baking sheet with parchment paper.
2. Slice eggplants into 1/2-inch rounds and place on the baking sheet.
3. In a bowl, mix olive oil, oregano, garlic powder, salt, and pepper. Brush both sides of eggplant slices with the mixture.
4. Roast in the oven for 20-25 mins until tender and golden brown.
5. Sprinkle feta cheese and Kalamata olives over the eggplant slices. Bake for 5 more mins until cheese melts.
6. Garnish with fresh parsley before serving.

Nutritional Information: Calories: 175 Protein: 6g Carbs: 12g Fat: 13g Fiber: 6g Cholesterol: 17mg Sodium: 347mg Potassium: 524mg

Cauliflower Tabbouleh Salad

Yield: 4 servings | **Prep time:** 15 minutes | **Cook time:** 0 minutes

Ingredients:

- 1 medium cauliflower head
- 1 cup chopped fresh parsley
- 1/2 cup chopped fresh mint
- 1/2 cup diced cucumber
- Salt and pepper, to taste
- 1/4 cup diced red onion
- 1/4 cup diced cherry tomatoes
- 2 tablespoons extra-virgin olive oil
- 2 tablespoons lemon juice

Directions:

1. Cut the cauliflower into florets and place them in a food processor. Pulse until the cauliflower resembles couscous-like texture.
2. Transfer the cauliflower "couscous" to a large mixing bowl.
3. Add the chopped parsley, mint, cucumber, red onion, and cherry tomatoes to the bowl with the cauliflower.
4. In a small bowl, whisk together the olive oil and lemon juice. Season with salt and pepper to taste.
5. Pour the dressing over the cauliflower mixture and toss until well combined.
6. Allow the salad to sit for about 10 minutes to let the flavors meld together.
7. Serve the cauliflower tabbouleh salad chilled or at room temperature.

Nutritional Information: Calories: 100 Protein: 4g Carbohydrates: 9g Fat: 7g Fiber: 4g Cholesterol: 0mg Sodium: 50mg Potassium: 481mg

Portobello Mushroom "Steaks" with Herbed Butter

Yield: 4 servings | **Prep time:** 10 minutes | **Cook time:** 15 minutes

Ingredients:

- 4 large Portobello mushrooms
- 4 tablespoons unsalted butter, softened
- 2 cloves garlic, minced
- Salt and pepper, to taste
- 2 tablespoons chopped fresh parsley
- 1 tablespoon chopped fresh thyme

Directions:

1. Preheat the grill or a grill pan over medium heat. Clean the Portobello mushrooms and remove the stems.
2. In a small bowl, combine the softened butter, minced garlic, chopped parsley, and chopped thyme. Season with salt and pepper to taste.
3. Spread the herbed butter mixture evenly on both sides of the Portobello mushrooms.
4. Place the mushrooms on the preheated grill or grill pan and cook for about 5-7 minutes per side, or until they are tender and slightly charred. Remove the mushrooms from the grill and let them rest for a few minutes before serving. Serve the Portobello mushroom "steaks" as a main dish or as a side dish with your favorite Mediterranean-inspired sides.

Nutritional Information: Calories: 140 Protein: 4g Carbohydrates: 4g Fat: 13g Fiber: 2g Cholesterol: 30mg Sodium: 10mg Potassium: 480mg

Greek Zucchini Fritters with Tzatziki Sauce

Yield: 4 servings | **Prep time:** 15 mins | **Cook time:** 15 mins

Ingredients: For the zucchini fritters:

- 2 medium zucchinis
- 2 green onions, finely chopped
- 2 cloves garlic, minced
- 1/4 cup chopped fresh dill
- Olive oil, for frying
- 1/4 cup chopped fresh parsley
- 1/4 cup almond flour
- 2 large eggs, beaten
- Salt and pepper, to taste

For the tzatziki sauce:

- 1/2 cup Greek yogurt
- 1/4 cup grated cucumber
- 1 clove garlic, minced
- Salt and pepper, to taste
- 1 tbsp lemon juice
- 1 tbsp chopped fresh dill

Directions:

1. Grate zucchinis and squeeze out excess moisture., In a bowl, combine zucchini, green onions, garlic, dill, parsley, almond flour, eggs, salt, and pepper. Heat olive oil in a skillet over medium heat.
2. Form small patties from the zucchini mixture and fry them in the skillet until golden brown and crispy.
3. In a bowl, mix Greek yogurt, grated cucumber, garlic, lemon juice, dill, salt, and pepper to make the tzatziki sauce. Serve the zucchini fritters with tzatziki sauce on top.

Nutritional Information: Calories: 160 Protein: 8g Carbohydrates: 8g Fat: 11g Fiber: 2g Cholesterol: 105mg Sodium: 220mg Potassium: 414mg

Spinach and Feta Stuffed Bell Peppers

Yield: 4 servings | **Prep time:** 15 mins | **Cook time:** 30 mins

Ingredients:

- 4 bell peppers
- 2 tbsp olive oil
- 1 small onion, diced
- 2 cloves garlic, minced
- Salt and pepper, to taste
- 4 cups chopped spinach
- 1/2 cup crumbled feta cheese
- 1/4 cup grated Parmesan cheese
- 1/4 tsp dried oregano

Directions:

1. Preheat the oven to 375°F (190°C). Grease a baking dish.
2. Slice off the tops of the bell peppers and remove the seeds.
3. In a skillet, sauté onion and garlic in olive oil until softened.
4. Add spinach to the skillet and cook until wilted. Remove from heat.
5. Mix spinach, feta cheese, Parmesan cheese, oregano, salt, and pepper in a bowl.
6. Stuff bell peppers with the spinach and feta mixture.
7. Place the stuffed bell peppers in the baking dish and bake for 25-30 minutes.
8. Let cool for a few minutes before serving.

Nutritional Information: Calories: 210 Protein: 8g Carbohydrates: 14g Fat: 14g Fiber: 4g Cholesterol: 25mg Sodium: 340mg Potassium: 591mg

Mediterranean Roasted Vegetable Salad

Yield: 4 servings | **Prep time:** 15 mins | **Cook time:** 25 mins

Ingredients:

- 2 zucchinis, sliced
- 1 eggplant, cubed
- 1 red bell pepper, sliced
- 1 yellow bell pepper, sliced
- 1 small red onion, thinly sliced
- 2 tbsp olive oil
- 2 cloves garlic, minced
- Juice of 1 lemon
- 1 tsp dried oregano
- Salt and pepper, to taste
- 4 cups mixed salad greens
- 1/4 cup Kalamata olives, halved
- 1/4 cup crumbled feta cheese
- 2 tbsp chopped fresh parsley

Directions:

1. Preheat oven to 425°F (220°C).
2. Toss zucchinis, eggplant, bell peppers, and red onion with olive oil, garlic, oregano, salt, and pepper in a baking dish.
3. Roast vegetables for 20-25 mins until tender and slightly browned.
4. Place mixed salad greens in a large bowl.
5. Add roasted vegetables to the bowl.
6. Top with Kalamata olives, feta cheese, parsley, and lemon juice. Gently toss to combine.
7. Serve as a main dish or side.

Nutritional Information: Calories: 180 Protein: 5g Carbohydrates: 15g Fat: 12g Fiber: 6g Cholesterol: 4mg Sodium: 220mg Potassium: 600mg

Lemon Garlic Broccoli with Toasted Almonds

Yield: 4 servings | **Prep time:** 10 mins | **Cook time:** 10 mins

Ingredients:

- 4 cups broccoli florets
- 2 tbsp olive oil
- 3 cloves garlic, minced
- 1/4 cup toasted sliced almonds
- Zest and juice of 1 lemon
- Salt and pepper, to taste

Directions:

1. Blanch the broccoli florets in salted boiling water for 2 minutes. Drain and set aside.
2. Heat olive oil in a skillet over medium heat. Sauté minced garlic for 1 minute.
3. Add the blanched broccoli to the skillet and toss with garlic-infused oil.
4. Squeeze lemon juice, sprinkle lemon zest, and season with salt and pepper.
5. Cook the broccoli for 3-4 minutes until crisp-tender and lightly browned.
6. Toast sliced almonds in a separate skillet until golden and fragrant.
7. Sprinkle toasted almonds over the cooked broccoli.
8. Serve as a side dish or main meal.

Nutritional Information: Calories: 120 Protein: 5g Carbohydrates: 9g Fat: 9g Fiber: 4g Cholesterol: 0mg Sodium: 80mg Potassium: 380mg

Ratatouille with Herbed Quinoa

Yield: 4 servings | **Prep time:** 15 mins | **Cook time:** 30 mins

Ingredients:

- 1 eggplant, diced
- 1 zucchini, diced
- 1 yellow squash, diced
- 1 red bell pepper, diced
- 1 yellow bell pepper, diced
- 1 small red onion, diced
- 3 cloves garlic, minced
- Fresh parsley and basil, chopped (for garnish)
- 2 tbsp olive oil
- 1 can (14 oz) diced tomatoes
- 2 tbsp tomato paste
- 1 tsp dried oregano
- 1 tsp dried basil
- Salt and pepper, to taste
- 1 cup cooked quinoa

Directions:

1. In a large skillet, sauté the diced eggplant, zucchini, yellow squash, red bell pepper, yellow bell pepper, red onion, and garlic in olive oil for 5 minutes.
2. Add diced tomatoes, tomato paste, dried oregano, dried basil, salt, and pepper. Stir and simmer for 20 minutes.
3. While the ratatouille is simmering, cook the quinoa according to package instructions.
4. Once the ratatouille is cooked and the vegetables are tender, remove from heat.
5. In a serving bowl, mix the cooked quinoa with fresh parsley and basil.
6. Serve the ratatouille over the herbed quinoa.
7. Garnish with additional fresh herbs, if desired.

Nutritional Information: Calories: 220 Protein: 6g Carbohydrates: 31g Fat: 9g Fiber: 8g Cholesterol: 0mg Sodium: 260mg Potassium: 800mg

Greek Salad with Avocado and Halloumi

Yield: 4 servings | **Prep time:** 15 minutes | **Cook time:** 10 minutes

Ingredients:

- 1 head romaine lettuce, chopped
- 1 English cucumber, diced
- 1 cup cherry tomatoes, halved
- 1/2 red onion, thinly sliced
- 1/2 cup Kalamata olives
- Salt and pepper, to taste
- 1 avocado, diced
- 8 oz halloumi cheese, sliced
- 2 tbsp olive oil
- 2 tbsp lemon juice
- 1 tsp dried oregano

Directions:

1. In a large salad bowl, combine the chopped romaine lettuce, diced cucumber, halved cherry tomatoes, thinly sliced red onion, Kalamata olives, and diced avocado.
2. Preheat a skillet over medium heat. Add the halloumi cheese slices and cook for 2-3 minutes on each side until golden brown.
3. Remove the cooked halloumi from the skillet and let it cool slightly. Cut the halloumi into bite-sized pieces.
4. Add the halloumi to the salad bowl with the other ingredients.
5. In a small bowl, whisk together olive oil, lemon juice, dried oregano, salt, and pepper to make the dressing.
6. Pour the dressing over the salad and toss gently to combine all the ingredients.
7. Serve the Greek salad with avocado and halloumi as a refreshing and satisfying meal.

Nutritional Information: Calories: 290 Protein: 13g Carbohydrates: 15g Fat: 21g Fiber: 8g Cholesterol: 40mg Sodium: 690mg Potassium: 610mg

Zucchini Noodles with Pesto and Cherry Tomatoes

Yield: 4 servings | **Prep time:** 15 mins | **Cook time:** 10 mins

Ingredients:

- 4 medium zucchini
- 1 cup cherry tomatoes, halved
- 1/4 cup pine nuts
- 2 cloves garlic
- Salt and pepper, to taste
- 2 cups fresh basil leaves
- 1/4 cup grated Parmesan cheese
- 1/4 cup extra virgin olive oil

Directions:

1. Make zucchini noodles using a spiralizer or vegetable peeler.
2. Toast pine nuts in a dry skillet until golden brown.
3. Blend pine nuts, garlic, basil leaves, Parmesan cheese, olive oil, salt, and pepper to make the pesto sauce.
4. In a skillet, sauté cherry tomatoes for 2-3 minutes.
5. Add zucchini noodles to the skillet and sauté for another 2-3 minutes.
6. Stir in the pesto sauce until noodles are coated.
7. Serve and enjoy!

Nutritional Information: Calories: 180 Protein: 6g Carbohydrates: 8g Fat: 16g Fiber: 3g Cholesterol: 4mg Sodium: 140mg Potassium: 520mg

Stuffed Artichokes with Herbed Breadcrumbs

Yield: 4 servings | **Prep time:** 20 mins | **Cook time:** 45 mins

Ingredients:

- 4 large artichokes
- 1 cup keto-friendly breadcrumbs
- 1/4 cup grated Parmesan cheese
- 2 cloves garlic, minced
- Salt and pepper, to taste
- 2 tbsp chopped fresh herbs (parsley, basil, thyme)
- 1/4 cup extra virgin olive oil

Directions:

1. Preheat the oven to 375°F (190°C).
2. Prepare artichokes by trimming the tops, removing tough outer leaves, and scooping out the choke.
3. In a bowl, mix breadcrumbs, Parmesan cheese, minced garlic, chopped herbs, olive oil, salt, and pepper.
4. Stuff the breadcrumb mixture into the artichokes.
5. Place the artichokes in a baking dish, drizzle with olive oil, and cover with foil.
6. Bake for 30 mins, then remove the foil and bake for an additional 15 mins until tender and breadcrumbs are golden.
7. Serve hot with lemon wedges.
8. Enjoy!

Nutritional Information: Calories: 220 Protein: 7g Carbohydrates: 21g Fat: 13g Fiber: 9g Cholesterol: 4mg Sodium: 350mg Potassium: 550mg

Cauliflower and Chickpea Curry

Yield: 4 servings | **Prep time:** 10 mins | **Cook time:** 30 mins

Ingredients:

- 1 head cauliflower, cut into florets
- 1 can chickpeas, drained
- 1 onion, chopped
- 3 cloves garlic, minced
- 1 tbsp curry powder
- 1 tsp ground cumin
- 1 tsp ground coriander
- Lemon wedges, for serving
- 1/2 tsp turmeric powder
- 1/4 tsp cayenne pepper (optional)
- 1 can diced tomatoes
- 1 cup coconut milk
- Salt and pepper, to taste
- Fresh cilantro, for garnish

Directions:

1. Sauté onion and garlic. Add cauliflower and cook for 5 mins.
2. Stir in spices. Add chickpeas, diced tomatoes, and coconut milk. Season with salt and pepper.
3. Simmer covered for 15-20 mins until cauliflower is tender.
4. Adjust seasoning if needed.
5. Serve over quinoa or cauliflower rice.
6. Garnish with cilantro and serve with lemon wedges.
7. Enjoy!

Nutritional Information: Calories: 250 Protein: 9g Carbohydrates: 28g Fat: 12g Fiber: 9g Cholesterol: 0mg Sodium: 500mg Potassium: 800mg

Mediterranean Stuffed Portobello Mushrooms

Yield: 4 servings | **Prep time:** 15 mins | **Cook time:** 20 mins

Ingredients:

- 4 large portobello mushrooms
- 1 tbsp olive oil
- 1 small onion, finely chopped
- 2 cloves garlic, minced
- 1/2 cup diced tomatoes
- Salt and pepper, to taste
- 1/4 cup chopped Kalamata olives
- 1/4 cup crumbled feta cheese
- 2 tbsp chopped fresh parsley
- 1 tbsp lemon juice

Directions:

1. Preheat oven to 375°F (190°C). Line a baking sheet with parchment paper.
2. Remove mushroom stems and scrape out gills.
3. Sauté onion and garlic in olive oil until softened.
4. Add tomatoes, cook for 2 mins, then remove from heat.
5. Stir in olives, feta, parsley, lemon juice, salt, and pepper.
6. Fill mushrooms with the mixture and place on baking sheet.
7. Bake for 15-20 mins until mushrooms are tender and filling is golden.
8. Let cool for a few minutes before serving.
9. Enjoy as a main course or with a salad.

Nutritional Information: Calories: 120 Protein: 7g Carbohydrates: 10g Fat: 7g Fiber: 3g Cholesterol: 6mg Sodium: 310mg Potassium: 560mg

Greek Spinach and Feta Stuffed Peppers

Yield: 4 servings | **Prep time:** 15 minutes | **Cook time:** 25 minutes

Ingredients:

- 4 large bell peppers (any color)
- 1 tbsp olive oil
- 1 small onion, finely chopped
- 2 cloves garlic, minced
- Salt and pepper, to taste
- 4 cups fresh spinach, chopped
- 1 cup crumbled feta cheese
- 1/4 cup chopped fresh dill

Directions:

1. Preheat the oven to 375°F (190°C).
2. Cut the tops off the bell peppers and remove the seeds and membranes.
3. Heat olive oil in a skillet over medium heat. Add onion and garlic, and sauté until softened.
4. Add spinach to the skillet and cook until wilted.
5. Remove from heat and stir in feta cheese and dill. Season with salt and pepper.
6. Stuff the bell peppers with the spinach and feta mixture.
7. Place the stuffed peppers in a baking dish and bake for 20-25 minutes, until the peppers are tender and the filling is heated through.
8. Remove from the oven and let cool for a few minutes before serving.

Nutritional Information: Calories: 170 Protein: 10g Carbohydrates: 12g Fat: 10g Fiber: 4g Cholesterol: 25mg Sodium: 480mg Potassium: 540mg

Grilled Halloumi and Vegetable Skewers

Yield: 4 servings | **Prep time:** 15 minutes | **Cook time:** 10 minutes

Ingredients:

- 8 ounces halloumi cheese, cut into cubes
- 1 zucchini, sliced
- 1 red bell pepper, cut into chunks
- 1 red onion, cut into chunks
- 8 cherry tomatoes
- Fresh parsley, for garnish (optional)
- 2 tablespoons olive oil
- 1 tablespoon lemon juice
- 1 teaspoon dried oregano
- Salt and pepper, to taste

Directions:

1. Preheat the grill to medium-high heat.
2. Thread the halloumi cheese, zucchini, bell pepper, red onion, and cherry tomatoes onto skewers.
3. In a small bowl, whisk together the olive oil, lemon juice, dried oregano, salt, and pepper.
4. Brush the skewers with the olive oil mixture, coating all sides.
5. Place the skewers on the grill and cook for about 4-5 minutes per side, until the vegetables are tender and the halloumi cheese is slightly charred. Remove the skewers from the grill and let them cool slightly.
6. Garnish with fresh parsley, if desired, and serve hot.

Nutritional Information: Calories: 220 Protein: 12g Carbohydrates: 9g Fat: 16g Fiber: 2g Cholesterol: 45mg Sodium: 480mg Potassium: 310mg

Mediterranean Roasted Cauliflower with Tahini Sauce

Yield: 4 servings | **Prep time:** 10 minutes | **Cook time:** 25 minutes

Ingredients:

- 1 head of cauliflower, cut into florets
- 2 tablespoons olive oil
- 1 teaspoon ground cumin
- 1 teaspoon ground paprika
- 1/2 teaspoon garlic powder
- 1 tablespoon chopped fresh parsley, for garnish (optional)
- Salt and pepper, to taste
- 2 tablespoons tahini
- 2 tablespoons lemon juice
- 2 tablespoons water

Directions:

1. Preheat oven to 425°F (220°C) and line a baking sheet with parchment paper.
2. Toss cauliflower florets with olive oil, cumin, paprika, garlic powder, salt, and pepper.
3. Spread cauliflower on the baking sheet and roast for 20-25 minutes.
4. Meanwhile, whisk tahini, lemon juice, water, and a pinch of salt in a small bowl.
5. Once cauliflower is roasted, drizzle with tahini sauce or serve as a dip.
6. Optional: Garnish with chopped parsley.
7. Serve warm.

Nutritional Information (per serving): Calories: 120 Protein: 4g Carbohydrates: 9g Fat: 9g Fiber: 4g Cholesterol: 0mg Sodium: 90mg Potassium: 480mg

Lemon Garlic Roasted Brussels Sprouts

Yield: 4 servings | **Prep time:** 10 minutes | **Cook time:** 20 minutes

Ingredients:

- 1 lb Brussels sprouts, trimmed and halved
- 2 tbsp olive oil
- 3 cloves garlic, minced
- Salt and pepper, to taste
- Zest of 1 lemon
- 1 tbsp lemon juice

Directions:

1. Preheat oven to 425°F (220°C) and line a baking sheet with parchment paper.
2. In a bowl, combine Brussels sprouts, olive oil, minced garlic, lemon zest, lemon juice, salt, and pepper. Toss until well coated.
3. Spread Brussels sprouts in a single layer on the baking sheet.
4. Roast in the preheated oven for 18-20 minutes, or until Brussels sprouts are tender and lightly browned.
5. Remove from the oven and serve hot.

Nutritional Information (per serving): Calories: 110 Protein: 4g Carbohydrates: 12g Fat: 7g Fiber: 4g Cholesterol: 0mg Sodium: 30mg Potassium: 500mg

Eggplant Parmesan with Zucchini Noodles

Yield: 4 servings | **Prep time:** 20 minutes | **Cook time:** 40 minutes

Ingredients:

- 1 large eggplant
- Salt
- 2 medium zucchini
- 1 cup marinara sauce
- 1 cup shredded mozzarella cheese
- 1/4 cup grated Parmesan cheese
- Salt and pepper
- 1/4 cup almond flour
- 1/4 cup chopped fresh basil
- 2 tbsp olive oil
- 2 cloves garlic, minced
- 1/2 tsp dried oregano

Directions:

1. Slice eggplant into rounds and salt both sides. Let sit for 15 minutes, rinse, and pat dry.
2. Spiralize or julienne zucchini into noodles.
3. Combine almond flour, grated Parmesan, oregano, salt, and pepper. Coat eggplant slices with the mixture.
4. Bake eggplant at 375°F (190°C) for 15 minutes.
5. In a skillet, sauté minced garlic in olive oil. Add zucchini noodles and cook for 3-4 minutes.
6. Layer marinara sauce, eggplant slices, and zucchini noodles in a baking dish. Top with marinara and mozzarella.
7. Bake for 20 minutes until cheese melts and bubbles.
8. Let cool, garnish with fresh basil, and serve.

Nutritional Information (per serving): Calories: 250 Protein: 12g Carbohydrates: 16g Fat: 16g Fiber: 8g Cholesterol: 25mg Sodium: 480mg Potassium: 750mg

Greek Lentil Soup with Spinach and Lemon

Yield: 4 servings | **Prep time:** 10 minutes | **Cook time:** 40 minutes

Ingredients:

- 1 cup green lentils
- 1 onion, chopped
- 2 cloves garlic, minced
- 2 carrots, diced
- 2 celery stalks, diced
- 4 cups vegetable broth
- Olive oil for drizzling
- 1 bay leaf
- 1 tsp dried oregano
- 1 tsp dried thyme
- 4 cups fresh spinach leaves
- Juice of 1 lemon
- Salt and pepper to taste

Directions:

1. Rinse the lentils under cold water and set aside.
2. In a large pot, heat olive oil over medium heat. Add the onion, garlic, carrots, and celery. Sauté until vegetables are tender.
3. Add the lentils, vegetable broth, bay leaf, oregano, and thyme to the pot. Bring to a boil, then reduce heat and simmer for 30 minutes or until lentils are cooked.
4. Stir in the spinach and cook for an additional 5 minutes until wilted.
5. Remove the bay leaf and stir in the lemon juice. Season with salt and pepper to taste.
6. Ladle the soup into bowls and drizzle with olive oil before serving.

Nutritional Information (per serving): Calories: 250 Protein: 15g Carbohydrates: 40g Fat: 4g Fiber: 15g Cholesterol: 0mg Sodium: 800mg Potassium: 1000mg

Roasted Asparagus with Feta and Lemon

Yield: 4 servings | **Prep time:** 5 minutes | **Cook time:** 15 minutes

Ingredients:

- 1 bunch asparagus
- 2 tbsp olive oil
- Salt and pepper to taste
- 1 lemon, zested and juiced
- 1/4 cup crumbled feta cheese

Directions:

1. Preheat the oven to 425°F (220°C).
2. Trim the tough ends of the asparagus spears.
3. Place the asparagus on a baking sheet and drizzle with olive oil. Toss to coat evenly.
4. Sprinkle the lemon zest over the asparagus and season with salt and pepper.
5. Roast in the preheated oven for 12-15 minutes or until the asparagus is tender and slightly charred.
6. Remove from the oven and drizzle with lemon juice.
7. Sprinkle the crumbled feta cheese over the asparagus.
8. Serve warm as a side dish or appetizer.

Nutritional Information (per serving): Calories: 90 Protein: 4g Carbohydrates: 4g Fat: 7g Fiber: 2g Cholesterol: 5mg Sodium: 120mg Potassium: 250mg

Desserts

Lemon Almond Ricotta Cake

Yield: 6 servings | **Prep time:** 15 minutes | **Cook time:** 40 minutes

Ingredients:

- 1 cup almond flour
- 1/2 cup coconut flour
- 1 teaspoon baking powder
- 1/4 teaspoon salt
- 4 large eggs
- 1/2 cup unsalted butter, melted
- 1 cup ricotta cheese
- 1/2 cup granulated erythritol (or any keto-friendly sweetener)
- 1 teaspoon vanilla extract
- Zest of 2 lemons
- 1/4 cup fresh lemon juice

Directions:

1. Preheat the oven to 350°F (175°C). Grease a 9-inch round cake pan with butter or cooking spray.
2. In a large bowl, combine the almond flour, coconut flour, baking powder, and salt. Mix well.
3. In another bowl, whisk together the eggs, melted butter, erythritol, vanilla extract, lemon zest, lemon juice, and ricotta cheese until well combined.
4. Gradually add the wet ingredients to the dry ingredients, mixing until a smooth batter forms.
5. Pour the batter into the prepared cake pan and spread it evenly.
6. Bake in the preheated oven for 35-40 minutes or until a toothpick inserted into the center comes out clean.
7. Remove the cake from the oven and let it cool in the pan for 10 minutes. Then, transfer it to a wire rack to cool completely before serving.

Nutritional Information: Approximately 240 calories, 9g protein, 8g carbohydrates, 20g fat, 3g fiber, 120mg cholesterol, 180mg sodium, 120mg potassium.

Raspberry Chia Pudding

Yield: 4 servings | **Prep time:** 5 minutes | **Cook time:** 0 minutes

Ingredients:

- 1 cup unsweetened almond milk
- 1 cup fresh raspberries
- 2 tablespoons chia seeds
- Optional toppings: additional raspberries, sliced almonds, shredded coconut
- 1 tablespoon keto-friendly sweetener (e.g., stevia, erythritol)
- 1/2 teaspoon vanilla extract

Directions:

1. Blend almond milk, raspberries, sweetener, and vanilla extract until smooth.
2. Pour mixture into a bowl or individual jars.
3. Whisk in chia seeds until well combined.
4. Refrigerate for at least 2 hours or overnight to thicken.
5. Stir before serving.
6. Top with raspberries, almonds, and coconut if desired.

Nutritional Information: Approximately 80 calories, 2g protein, 7g carbohydrates, 5g fat, 5g fiber, 0mg cholesterol, 60mg sodium, 120mg potassium.

Chocolate Avocado Mousse

Yield: 4 servings | **Prep time:** 10 minutes | **Cook time:** 0 minutes

Ingredients:

- 2 ripe avocados
- 1/4 cup unsweetened cocoa powder
- 1/4 cup keto-friendly sweetener (e.g., stevia, erythritol)
- 1/4 cup unsweetened almond milk
- 1 teaspoon vanilla extract
- Pinch of salt
- Optional toppings: whipped cream, shaved dark chocolate, fresh berries

Directions:

1. Cut the avocados in half, remove the pit, and scoop out the flesh into a blender or food processor.
2. Add the cocoa powder, sweetener, almond milk, vanilla extract, and salt to the blender.
3. Blend until all the ingredients are well combined and the mixture is smooth and creamy.
4. Taste and adjust the sweetness if desired by adding more sweetener.
5. Transfer the chocolate avocado mousse to serving bowls or glasses.
6. Refrigerate for at least 1 hour to chill and set.
7. Before serving, add optional toppings such as whipped cream, shaved dark chocolate, or fresh berries.

Nutritional Information: Approximately 150 calories, 3g protein, 9g carbohydrates, 12g fat, 7g fiber, 0mg cholesterol, 70mg sodium, 480mg potassium.

Pistachio Rosewater Semolina Cookies

Yield: 12 servings | **Prep time:** 15 minutes | **Cook time:** 12 minutes

Ingredients:

- 1 cup fine semolina flour
- 1/2 cup almond flour
- 1/2 cup finely chopped unsalted pistachios
- 1/4 cup keto-friendly sweetener
- Optional: additional pistachios for garnish
- 1/4 cup melted coconut oil
- 2 tbsp rosewater
- 1 tsp baking powder
- 1/4 tsp salt

Directions:

1. Preheat oven to 350°F (175°C) and line a baking sheet with parchment paper.
2. In a bowl, combine semolina flour, almond flour, chopped pistachios, sweetener, baking powder, and salt.
3. Add melted coconut oil and rosewater, and mix until a dough forms.
4. Roll portions of the dough into balls and place on the baking sheet. Flatten slightly.
5. Optionally, garnish with a whole pistachio on each cookie.
6. Bake for 10-12 minutes until edges are golden brown.
7. Let cool on the baking sheet before transferring to a wire rack.

Nutritional Information: Approximately 110 calories, 3g protein, 9g carbohydrates, 8g fat, 1g fiber, 0mg cholesterol, 60mg sodium, 85mg potassium.

Coconut Lime Energy Balls

Yield: 12 servings | **Prep time:** 15 minutes | **Cook time:** 0 minutes

Ingredients:

- 1 cup unsweetened shredded coconut
- 1/2 cup almond flour
- 1/4 cup coconut oil, melted
- 2 tablespoons lime juice
- Pinch of salt
- 1 tablespoon lime zest
- 2 tablespoons keto-friendly sweetener (e.g., stevia, erythritol)
- 1/2 teaspoon vanilla extract

Directions:

1. In a food processor, combine shredded coconut, almond flour, melted coconut oil, lime juice, lime zest, sweetener, vanilla extract, and salt.
2. Pulse the mixture until it comes together and forms a sticky dough.
3. Scoop out tablespoon-sized portions of the dough and roll them into balls.
4. Place the coconut lime energy balls on a baking sheet lined with parchment paper.
5. Refrigerate the energy balls for at least 1 hour to firm up.
6. Once chilled, the energy balls are ready to be enjoyed. Store any leftovers in an airtight container in the refrigerator.

Nutritional Information: Approximately 110 calories, 1g protein, 4g carbohydrates, 10g fat, 2g fiber, 0mg cholesterol, 25mg sodium, 70mg potassium.

Greek Yogurt Parfait with Berries and Nuts

Yield: 4 servings | **Prep time:** 10 minutes | **Cook time:** 0 minutes

Ingredients:

- 2 cups Greek yogurt (unsweetened)
- 1 cup mixed berries (e.g., strawberries, blueberries, raspberries)
- 1 teaspoon vanilla extract
- 1/4 cup chopped nuts (e.g., almonds, walnuts, pistachios)
- 2 tablespoons keto-friendly sweetener (e.g., stevia, erythritol)

Directions:

1. In a bowl, combine Greek yogurt, sweetener, and vanilla extract. Mix well.
2. Layer a portion of the yogurt mixture in the bottom of serving glasses or bowls.
3. Add a layer of mixed berries on top of the yogurt.
4. Sprinkle a portion of chopped nuts over the berries.
5. Repeat the layers with the remaining yogurt, berries, and nuts.
6. Finish with a final sprinkle of nuts on top.
7. Serve immediately or refrigerate until ready to enjoy.

Nutritional Information: Approximately 160 calories, 12g protein, 10g carbohydrates, 8g fat, 2g fiber, 10mg cholesterol, 60mg sodium, 260mg potassium.

Orange Olive Oil Cake

Yield: 8 servings | **Prep time:** 15 minutes | **Cook time:** 40 minutes

Ingredients:

- 2 medium oranges
- 4 large eggs
- 1/2 cup keto-friendly sweetener
- 1/2 cup olive oil
- Optional: powdered sweetener for dusting
- 2 cups almond flour
- 1 tsp baking powder
- 1/4 tsp salt

Directions:

1. Preheat oven to 350°F (175°C) and grease a 9-inch round cake pan.
2. Boil oranges for 15 minutes, then cool, halve, and remove any seeds.
3. Blend cooked oranges (including peel) until smooth.
4. In a mixing bowl, beat eggs and sweetener. Add olive oil and blended oranges, and mix well.
5. In a separate bowl, combine almond flour, baking powder, and salt.
6. Gradually add dry ingredients to wet ingredients, stirring until smooth.
7. Pour batter into greased cake pan and smooth the top.
8. Bake for 35-40 minutes, or until a toothpick comes out clean.
9. Let the cake cool in the pan for 10 minutes, then transfer to a wire rack to cool completely.
10. Optional: Dust with powdered sweetener before serving.

Nutritional Information: Approximately 220 calories, 7g protein, 8g carbohydrates, 18g fat, 3g fiber, 80mg cholesterol, 120mg sodium, 170mg potassium.

Cinnamon Cardamom Almond Butter Cups

Yield: 12 servings | **Prep time:** 15 minutes | **Cook time:** 0 minutes

Ingredients:

- 1 cup almond butter (unsweetened)
- 1/4 cup coconut oil, melted
- 2 tablespoons keto-friendly sweetener (e.g., stevia, erythritol)
- Pinch of salt
- 1 teaspoon ground cinnamon
- 1/2 teaspoon ground cardamom
- 1/4 teaspoon vanilla extract

Directions:

1. In a bowl, combine almond butter, melted coconut oil, sweetener, ground cinnamon, ground cardamom, vanilla extract, and salt. Mix until well combined.
2. Line a muffin tin with paper or silicone cupcake liners.
3. Spoon a tablespoon of the almond butter mixture into each cupcake liner, smoothing the top.
4. Place the muffin tin in the refrigerator and chill for at least 1 hour, or until the almond butter cups are firm.
5. Once chilled and firm, remove the almond butter cups from the muffin tin and store them in an airtight container in the refrigerator.

Nutritional Information: Approximately 140 calories, 4g protein, 4g carbohydrates, 12g fat, 2g fiber, 0mg cholesterol, 25mg sodium, 180mg potassium.

Walnut Fig Bites

Yield: 12 servings | **Prep time:** 15 minutes | **Cook time:** 0 minutes

Ingredients:

- 1 cup walnuts
- 1 cup dried figs
- 2 tablespoons unsweetened almond butter
- Pinch of salt
- 1 tablespoon coconut flour
- 1 teaspoon ground cinnamon
- 1/4 teaspoon vanilla extract

Directions:

1. In a food processor, combine walnuts, dried figs, almond butter, coconut flour, ground cinnamon, vanilla extract, and salt.
2. Pulse the mixture until well combined and a sticky dough forms.
3. Scoop out tablespoon-sized portions of the dough and roll them into bite-sized balls.
4. Place the walnut fig bites on a plate or baking sheet lined with parchment paper.
5. Refrigerate the bites for at least 1 hour to firm up.
6. Once chilled, the walnut fig bites are ready to be enjoyed. Store any leftovers in an airtight container in the refrigerator.

Nutritional Information: Approximately 120 calories, 2g protein, 12g carbohydrates, 8g fat, 3g fiber, 0mg cholesterol, 5mg sodium, 180mg potassium

Almond Flour Chocolate Chip Cookies

Yield: 12 servings | **Prep time:** 10 minutes | **Cook time:** 12 minutes

Ingredients:

- 2 cups almond flour
- 1/4 cup coconut oil, melted
- 1/4 cup keto-friendly sweetener (e.g., stevia, erythritol)
- 1/2 cup sugar-free dark chocolate chips
- 1 teaspoon vanilla extract
- 1/4 teaspoon baking soda
- 1/4 teaspoon salt

Directions:

1. Preheat the oven to 350°F (175°C) and line a baking sheet with parchment paper.
2. In a mixing bowl, combine almond flour, melted coconut oil, sweetener, vanilla extract, baking soda, and salt. Mix well until a dough forms.
3. Fold in the sugar-free dark chocolate chips and mix until evenly distributed.
4. Scoop tablespoon-sized portions of dough and place them on the prepared baking sheet, spacing them apart.
5. Flatten each cookie slightly with the back of a spoon or your hand.
6. Bake in the preheated oven for 10-12 minutes, or until the edges turn golden brown.
7. Remove from the oven and let the cookies cool on the baking sheet for a few minutes, then transfer them to a wire rack to cool completely.

Nutritional Information: Approximately 160 calories, 4g protein, 6g carbohydrates, 14g fat, 2g fiber, 0mg cholesterol, 75mg sodium, 90mg potassium.

Pomegranate Coconut Panna Cotta

Yield: 4 servings | **Prep time:** 10 minutes | **Cook time:** 10 minutes | **Chill time:** 4 hours

Ingredients:

- 1 cup coconut milk
- 1 cup heavy cream
- 1/4 cup keto-friendly sweetener
- 2 tsp gelatin powder
- Fresh mint leaves
- 1/4 cup cold water
- 1 tsp vanilla extract
- 1/2 cup pomegranate arils

Directions:

1. In a saucepan, heat coconut milk, heavy cream, and sweetener until simmering.
2. In a small bowl, sprinkle gelatin over cold water and let it soften.
3. Remove the saucepan from heat and stir in the dissolved gelatin and vanilla extract.
4. Divide the mixture among serving glasses and refrigerate for 4 hours to set.
5. Garnish with pomegranate arils and mint leaves.
6. Serve chilled.

Nutritional Information: Approximately 320 calories, 4g protein, 6g carbohydrates, 32g fat, 0g fiber, 90mg cholesterol, 20mg sodium, 190mg potassium.

Hazelnut Chocolate Truffles

Yield: 12 servings | **Prep time:** 15 minutes | **Cook time:** 0 minutes | **Chill time:** 2 hours

Ingredients:

- 1 cup hazelnuts
- 1/4 cup unsweetened cocoa powder
- 1/4 cup powdered erythritol (or your preferred keto-friendly sweetener)
- 2 tablespoons coconut oil, melted
- 1 teaspoon vanilla extract
- Pinch of salt
- Optional: Additional cocoa powder or chopped hazelnuts for coating

Directions:

1. In a food processor, pulse the hazelnuts until finely ground.
2. Add the cocoa powder, powdered erythritol, melted coconut oil, vanilla extract, and salt to the food processor. Process until the mixture comes together into a sticky dough.
3. Transfer the mixture to a bowl and refrigerate for about 1 hour, or until firm.
4. Once the mixture is chilled and firm, use your hands to roll it into small truffle-sized balls.
5. Optional: Roll the truffles in additional cocoa powder or chopped hazelnuts to coat them.
6. Place the truffles on a baking sheet lined with parchment paper and refrigerate for another hour to set.
7. Serve the Hazelnut Chocolate Truffles chilled.

Nutritional Information: Approximately 120 calories, 2g protein, 4g carbohydrates, 11g fat, 2g fiber, 0mg cholesterol, 0mg sodium, 0mg potassium.

Blackberry Almond Crumble Bars

Yield: 9 servings | **Prep time:** 15 minutes | **Cook time:** 30 minutes

Ingredients:

- 2 cups almond flour
- 1/4 cup coconut flour
- 1/4 cup keto-friendly sweetener
- 1/2 tsp baking powder
- Optional: Additional sweetener for dusting
- 1/4 tsp salt
- 1/2 cup melted unsalted butter
- 1 tsp vanilla extract
- 1 1/2 cups fresh blackberries

Directions:

1. Preheat oven to 350°F (175°C) and line an 8x8-inch baking dish with parchment paper.
2. In a bowl, mix almond flour, coconut flour, sweetener, baking powder, and salt.
3. Stir in melted butter and vanilla extract to form a crumbly dough.
4. Press two-thirds of the dough into the baking dish for the crust.
5. Spread blackberries evenly over the crust.
6. Sprinkle remaining dough as a crumble topping.
7. Optional: Dust the top with extra sweetener.
8. Bake for 25-30 minutes until golden brown and bubbly.
9. Cool completely before cutting into squares.
10. Serve at room temperature.

Nutritional Information: Approximately 215 calories, 5g protein, 9g carbohydrates, 18g fat, 3g fiber, 20mg cholesterol, 70mg sodium, 160mg potassium.

Lemon Poppy Seed Muffins

Yield: 12 servings | **Prep time:** 10 minutes | **Cook time:** 20 minutes

Ingredients:

- 2 cups almond flour
- 1/4 cup coconut flour
- 1/4 cup keto-friendly sweetener
- 1 tsp baking powder
- 1/4 tsp salt
- 2 tbsp poppy seeds
- Zest of 1 lemon
- 3 tbsp lemon juice
- 1/4 cup melted unsalted butter
- 4 large eggs

Directions:

1. Preheat the oven to 350°F (175°C) and line a muffin tin with paper liners.
2. In a large bowl, mix almond flour, coconut flour, sweetener, baking powder, salt, and lemon zest.
3. In a separate bowl, whisk together lemon juice, melted butter, and eggs.
4. Add the wet ingredients to the dry ingredients and stir until well combined.
5. Fold in the poppy seeds. Divide the batter evenly among the muffin cups.
6. Bake for 18-20 minutes, or until the tops are golden and a toothpick inserted into the center comes out clean.
7. Allow the muffins to cool in the pan for a few minutes, then transfer them to a wire rack to cool completely.

Nutritional Information: Approximately 180 calories, 7g protein, 6g carbohydrates, 15g fat, 3g fiber, 90mg cholesterol, 120mg sodium, 100mg potassium.

Cardamom Pistachio Biscotti

Yield: 12 servings | **Prep time:** 15 mins | **Cook time:** 30 mins

Ingredients:

- 1 ¾ cups almond flour
- ½ cup unsalted pistachios, chopped
- ¼ cup keto sweetener
- 1 tsp ground cardamom
- 1 tsp vanilla extract
- ½ tsp baking powder
- ¼ tsp salt
- 2 large eggs

Directions:

1. Preheat oven to 325°F (165°C). Line a baking sheet with parchment paper.
2. Combine almond flour, pistachios, sweetener, cardamom, baking powder, and salt in a bowl.
3. Whisk eggs and vanilla extract in a separate bowl. Add to the dry ingredients and mix to form a dough.
4. Transfer the dough onto the baking sheet and shape into a 10x4-inch log.
5. Bake for 20-25 minutes until firm and lightly golden. Let it cool for 10 minutes.
6. Reduce oven temperature to 300°F (150°C). Slice the log diagonally into ½-inch thick biscotti.
7. Place biscotti cut side down on the baking sheet and bake for 10-12 minutes until crispy.
8. Cool completely on a wire rack.

Nutritional Information: Approx. 140 calories, 5g protein, 6g carbs, 12g fat, 2g fiber, 40mg cholesterol, 45mg sodium, 120mg potassium.

Coconut Flour Blueberry Pancakes

Yield: 4 servings | **Prep time:** 10 minutes | **Cook time:** 10 minutes

Ingredients:

- ½ cup coconut flour
- 4 large eggs
- ¼ cup unsweetened almond milk
- 2 tbsp keto sweetener
- Coconut oil for cooking
- 1 tsp baking powder
- ½ tsp vanilla extract
- ¼ tsp salt
- ½ cup fresh blueberries

Directions:

1. In a mixing bowl, whisk together the coconut flour, eggs, almond milk, sweetener, baking powder, vanilla extract, and salt until smooth.
2. Gently fold in the fresh blueberries into the batter.
3. Heat a non-stick skillet or griddle over medium heat and melt a small amount of coconut oil.
4. Scoop about ¼ cup of the batter onto the skillet for each pancake. Cook until bubbles form on the surface, then flip and cook for another 1-2 minutes until golden brown.
5. Repeat the process with the remaining batter, adding more coconut oil to the skillet as needed.
6. Serve the pancakes warm with your favorite keto-friendly toppings such as sugar-free maple syrup, additional blueberries, or a dollop of Greek yogurt.

Nutritional Information: Approx. 130 calories, 6g protein, 9g carbs, 7g fat, 6g fiber, 180mg cholesterol, 240mg sodium, 200mg potassium.

Orange Almond Biscotti

Yield: 12 servings | **Prep time:** 15 minutes | **Cook time:** 35 minutes

Ingredients:

- 2 cups almond flour
- ½ cup erythritol (or keto sweetener)
- 2 tbsp coconut flour
- 1 tsp baking powder
- ¼ tsp salt
- ¼ cup chopped almonds
- Zest of 1 orange
- 2 large eggs
- 1 tsp vanilla extract
- 1 tsp almond extract

Directions:

1. Preheat oven to 325°F (165°C) and line a baking sheet with parchment paper.
2. In a bowl, mix almond flour, erythritol, coconut flour, baking powder, salt, and orange zest.
3. In a separate bowl, whisk eggs, vanilla extract, and almond extract.
4. Add wet ingredients to dry ingredients and mix well to form a dough.
5. Fold in chopped almonds. Transfer dough to the baking sheet and shape into a 12x4-inch rectangular log.
6. Bake for 20-25 minutes until firm and lightly golden.
7. Cool for 10 minutes, then reduce oven temperature to 300°F (150°C).
8. Slice the log into ½-inch thick diagonal slices.
9. Place slices back on the baking sheet, cut side down, and bake for 10-12 minutes until crispy.
10. Cool completely before serving.

Nutritional Information: Approx. 120 calories, 5g protein, 6g carbohydrates, 9g fat, 3g fiber, 30mg cholesterol, 90mg sodium, 100mg potassium.

Strawberry Chia Seed Jam

Yield: 8 servings | **Prep time:** 5 minutes | **Cook time:** 20 minutes

Ingredients:

- 2 cups fresh strawberries, hulled and chopped
- 2 tbsp chia seeds
- 1 tsp lemon juice
- 1-2 tbsp keto sweetener (such as erythritol or stevia), to taste

Directions:

1. In a saucepan, combine the chopped strawberries, chia seeds, and keto sweetener.
2. Cook over medium heat, stirring occasionally, until the strawberries begin to soften and release their juices, about 5 minutes. Mash the strawberries with a fork or potato masher to desired consistency.
3. Continue cooking for another 10-15 minutes, stirring frequently, until the mixture thickens.
4. Remove from heat and stir in lemon juice.
5. Allow the jam to cool for a few minutes, then transfer it to a jar or container.
6. Let it cool completely at room temperature, then refrigerate for at least 1 hour to allow the jam to thicken further.
7. Serve the strawberry chia seed jam on keto-friendly bread, muffins, or use it as a topping for yogurt or pancakes.

Nutritional Information: Approximately 25 calories, 1g protein, 3g carbohydrates, 1g fat, 2g fiber, 0mg cholesterol, 0mg sodium, 70mg potassium.

Greek Yogurt Lemon Bars

Yield: 8 servings | **Prep time:** 15 minutes | **Cook time:** 25 minutes

Ingredients:

- 1 cup almond flour
- 1/4 cup coconut flour
- 1/4 cup powdered keto sweetener
- 1/4 tsp salt
- Optional: additional powdered sweetener for dusting
- 1/2 cup melted unsalted butter
- 1 cup Greek yogurt
- 3 large eggs
- Zest and juice of 1 lemon

Directions:

1. Preheat oven to 350°F (175°C) and line an 8x8-inch baking dish with parchment paper.
2. In a bowl, mix almond flour, coconut flour, powdered sweetener, and salt.
3. Stir in melted butter until the mixture resembles coarse crumbs.
4. Press mixture into the baking dish to form the crust.
5. Bake crust for 10 minutes until lightly golden.
6. In a separate bowl, whisk together Greek yogurt, eggs, lemon zest, lemon juice, and powdered sweetener.
7. Pour lemon filling over the baked crust.
8. Return to the oven and bake for 15 minutes until the filling is set.
9. Let it cool completely, then refrigerate for at least 2 hours.
10. Cut into squares and dust with powdered sweetener, if desired.

Nutritional Information: Approx. 140 calories, 5g protein, 5g carbohydrates, 11g fat, 2g fiber, 80mg cholesterol, 75mg sodium, 100mg potassium.

Almond Flour Pumpkin Bread

Yield: 8 servings | **Prep time:** 15 min | **Cook time:** 45 min

Ingredients:

- 2 cups almond flour
- 1/4 cup coconut flour
- 1/2 cup keto sweetener
- 2 tsp baking powder
- 1 tsp cinnamon
- 1/2 tsp nutmeg
- Optional: chopped walnuts or pecans for topping
- 1/4 tsp cloves
- 1/4 tsp salt
- 4 large eggs
- 1 cup pumpkin puree
- 1/4 cup melted coconut oil
- 1 tsp vanilla extract

Directions:

1. Preheat oven to 350°F (175°C) and line a loaf pan with parchment paper.
2. In a large bowl, whisk almond flour, coconut flour, sweetener, baking powder, spices, and salt.
3. In another bowl, whisk eggs, pumpkin puree, melted coconut oil, and vanilla extract.
4. Combine wet and dry ingredients, and mix well.
5. Pour batter into the prepared loaf pan, and top with nuts if desired.
6. Bake for 40-45 min or until a toothpick comes out clean.
7. Let cool in the pan for 10 min, then transfer to a wire rack to cool.

Nutritional Information: Approx. 180 cal, 7g protein, 7g carbs, 15g fat, 3g fiber, 70mg cholesterol, 180mg sodium, 200mg potassium.

Manufactured by Amazon.ca
Acheson, AB